Philosophy of an Introvert

Justin Reynolds

Published by Justin Reynolds, 2020.

While every precaution has been taken in the preparation of this book, the publisher assumes no responsibility for errors or omissions, or for damages resulting from the use of the information contained herein.

PHILOSOPHY OF AN INTROVERT

First edition. November 28, 2020.

Copyright © 2020 Justin Reynolds.

ISBN: 978-0578922676

Written by Justin Reynolds.

Table of Contents

Intro 1
The reinvention of humanity through an age of technology 3
The human psyche is the most chaotic, yet beautiful window to perceive life through 9
Pain and suffering is a natural part in seeing the grace of life 21
The world isn't black and white 27
Hope & Faith 33
Imagination-something this title lacks 39
Let's talk about love and relationships, shall we? 47
Mental Health 55
What place does heroism actually have among humankind? 63
Discovering the world outside of you reveals your level of influence on it-An encouragement to travel abroad 73
Now on to a less than stellar topic to keep you awake. Politics: an essential yet also silly part of civil society 81
The intricacies of word choice can sometimes be an enigma 91
Growth is an infinite endeavor in becoming the person you want to be throughout life 99
I learned what it truly means to be family after having mine annoy me for decades, just so I could write this for you. You're welcome. 107
A commentary on religion from an unconventional Christian 117
Can humans truly evolve? 129

An infinite cycle of death and rebirth is what colors in the circle of life 137
The One True Multiverse 145

Thank you to my Mother, Father, and younger brother, in addition to the rest of my family and friends. You have always been the best of me

Intro

Okay, so I feel like there's little point in wasting *too* much time with introductions. The entirety of this book is exactly what the title says it is after all. By design I'm a pretty introverted person, but I also have enough opinions about *things* in general that I figured I'd write a book about a few of them. Truth be told I don't have a fancy backstory to throw at you about who I am, although I will say I've always been a pretty odd person even as a kid (which I'll admit resulted in me coming off as pretty annoying to a lot of people who knew me back then, so if any of them are reading this, I solemnly apologize...for being annoying, not weird that is, I'm still pretty weird). Yeah, like, for instance, I often use steak knives to cut things you're not supposed to cut with steak knives...like apples. Anyway, despite my preference to remain closed off from people, I've also been gifted experiences that have shown me how nuanced humanity is, along with the varying realities we influence in our lifetimes. It's because of that I genuinely enjoy reflecting on things like the human condition and all the ways it connects with our larger worlds and the universe as a whole. Everything from meme culture to religion to multiverse theory if I'm being honest. Of course, I've also found philosophy on such topics is best absorbed when you know not to take it 100% seriously, or at least that's what I think given my own subjectivity. In some way, shape or form, you could argue all of my hot takes in this book are conjecture, but in the end the point isn't so much to persuade you than it is to give attention to some of the more *abstract* layers of these different life topics I believe are worth pondering over, whether you agree with them or not. All in all, I like thinking about humans, the fact that we existed in a vast universe, and all the ways we try to have a little fun while doing it. Thoughts like that that are worth staying up all night over, or writing books about, I guess.

The reinvention of humanity through an age of technology

So much can be said about the current digital age that it's hard to pinpoint the most significant things to talk about first. When you really think about it, the rate of technological advancement has risen exponentially within the last few decades. I think few disagree that acknowledging this helps us see just how *new* most of this innovation still is to humanity, ultimately yielding unforeseen consequences both good *and* bad on humankind. Some of which we've already seen of course, but there's a lot we're still merely predicting.

Regardless, most of the technology we utilize today is so heavily ingrained into our lives that we perceive much of it as essential, myself included. It's a common theme I've found to question just how far this new prosperity will take us in the long run of human history. I'm my estimate, our conceptualization of reality has undoubtedly been altered in terms of what our minds indulge in and give meaning to. Generally speaking, plenty of recent innovations started with simple premises have led us to live vicariously through intangible interactions, expressions, and simulations, pretty much reshaping what being human even looks like in some environments. Things like social media, cryptocurrency, automation, and probably most notoriously the use and evolution of smartphones just to name a few. They all contribute in forming these digital dimensions we reside in pretty much on the daily, steadily bleeding out into the real world with the refinement of physical infrastructures. What's funny is I can recall how mind-blowing a lot of innovations were to me when I was a kid. Flip phones were honestly the most entertaining gadgets to me for the longest time, and my favorite thing to do on mine was to play Tetris for hours on end (even now I'm a self-proclaimed master of the game). I also remember wanting to own a Sidekick when those were popular, shoutout to anyone who actually remembers those bad boys.

The turning point for me at least was definitely the ascension of the iPhone though. By the time Apple came out with a couple iterations, I was fascinated that such technology could just be carried around on the daily, and it really represented the pinnacle of what human beings are capable of creating (at least to kid me). Looking back, I don't think anyone deeply contemplated the concept of the average joe having a digital footprint over their lifetime. Even now, it's a surreal reality given how young much of today's inventions are.

In a way, it's really a double-edged sword when we're talking about humanity. On one hand, there's probably never been as many efficient modes to accomplish any given task in history as there is now, which is great. On the other hand, it's not hard to see that, despite becoming so heavily interconnected with ourselves and our environments, we're more separated in some ways than we ever have been as humans. Trust me, whatever human desire you could want, odds are there's an artificial version of it that you can either buy or just find online and be content with that. I'm not saying this is inherently bad, but it is holding a growing influence on how we perceive life and the universe as time goes on. One that goes beyond just having your phone out at the dinner table honestly. Much of our social constructs have evolved to a point where the only authentic connection some people have with each other is through the digital interactions they share, and in my view, this holds true in a global sense. On a deeper level, I think we're starting to question the significance behind what's naturally inherent to us when it comes to human behavior, versus what we can just artificially program or teach to ourselves through science and technology. I think it's a question of, *how essential* is such innovation in propelling the human race?

What's interesting is that in our race toward refinement under the reason of necessity, we often ignore the matter of *sustainability* when it comes to just about everything. See, I don't think it's a stretch to say that the exponential advancements of society far outpace our collective psychology as a species in trying to adapt to them. In making these innovations a part of who we are, we've inadvertently gone against our evolutionary nature in a plethora of ways. Honestly though, I don't see this as some sort of detrimental flaw destined to ruin us. What I do see is a lack of concern over how sustainable our integration with tech is. When we implement changes in society claiming that they are the future, it often (though not always) comes off the heels of present market/consumer demand, in what are essentially short time spans. We develop new technologies in short increments, always making sure they grant short term satisfaction in our societies, yet rarely consider the long term meaning of their integration into lives. I think that's part of the reason why so much of the daily devices and even software we use feel obsolete after only a few years. Obsolete not just in functionality, but also in meaning and fulfillment. The drive behind their inception doesn't account for the long game in life. I think as a species we're very much in a transitionary period in history where our minds, and in turn our collective psyches, have yet to adapt to the rapid changes in this world, contributing to such sentiments of meaninglessness.

Another contributor of this lies in how revamped the duality of information is in this modern world. Along with every kind of innovation have come networks (beyond just social media) to connect them. Cloud services, search engines, online storage, the millions of digital user accounts for any business or organization, even the evolution of the global news cycle, they all makeup not only our identities, but also influence their worth on a variety of levels. There's not only the individual, but then there's also the *persona* of that individual which is almost immortalized in a way when you think about it. If you posted a video of yourself acting a certain way ten years ago, that persona, while perhaps not a reflection of your current self, exists on its own now. That persona has the power to influence people for better *or* worse. I mean, just think of your ability to do a google search on any formerly living activist, or in turn dictator as an example.

Now, on a higher level, you also have the identities of modern businesses branded as living entities. Companies like Google, Twitter, Facebook, Samsung, Apple—we treat them as conscious, contemplative beings rather than groups of people running an organization. Over the years there have been countless debates and theories on whether these kinds of companies hold too much power, if they're abusing privacy, or even if they act too virtuous at times. Regardless, while the true realities of those matters are definitely important, it's also worth noting that such conglomerates are also changing the way we think about our collective knowledge as a species. It seems trivial to cite the change from paperback books in a library to digital documentation, but it becomes astonishing when you consider how, in addition to immortalizing certain ideas and personas, the shift over these past few decades has yielded repercussions very few anticipated. I mean, when you really ponder over it, it's easy to see how our ancestors from as early as fifty years ago probably imagined little of the modern world. It ultimately comes down to a slow redefine of what it means to be human.

Artificial intelligence is also the hot topic I feel many people cite as the final extension of this. At its core, AI really represents the collective consciousness of the human race interacting with, and interpreting reality through digital mediums. Despite it's obvious benefits to society, I think many people act skeptical of it in the same way people were once skeptical about science centuries ago, often referring to it as witchcraft when it came to factual things that went against religious belief. That's comparable to today when we pose such controversial questions about not just AI, but technology in general as our conversations become more and more introspective. Questions like whether or not companies and AI will grow to outpace the basic capabilities of humans for instance. We grow fearful over imagining this, yet I honestly don't think an apocalyptic future will come to pass like in the movies. That's not to say such fears are unwarranted however. When I look at the way we've grown to treat companies as entities that can act on their own, I'd say a future where we look at AI in the same manner also has possibility.

At the root of all this lies a significant correlation between the concept/act of creation and technology. That essence has always been connected with human life, and it's been refined more than ever in today's digital age. Simply put, our capability of creation is limited, and we naturally seek to push the boundaries of that limit, just as we do with everything else we are. Honestly, I think one of the *greatest* abilities humans have developed over the past century or so, and especially in the digital age, is our ability of foresight. It's encompassed by our knack to predict the future based on a number of variables, all interwoven with probability. Despite my earlier comment that we're *merely* predicting consequences in modern day, such a small factor in our human thinking, while limited as I said, has always been a driving force behind these simulations we create in our minds for the future. The visions we have, whether for change or just prophecy, are one of the most important factors that help propel humanity past all the useless clutter technology may leave us with. Ultimately, when it comes to where humankind stands at the moment, we're looking at an absurd number of potential futures for how things play out in the long run of our time in this life. Pay attention to the overlap between the many factors involved, and you'll see life becomes *a lot* more interesting.

The human psyche is the most chaotic, yet beautiful window to perceive life through

It's an interesting thought to behold that in the course of human history, billions upon billions of individual perspectives of the world and its inhabitants have existed. In hindsight, the human race has only existed for a short time, yet the ways we process life around us has evolved dramatically. Centuries have seen the psychology of our minds undergo constant reinvention, and I doubt many would dispute that the upper limits of what we're capable of engaging with have been anything but a linear progression. Despite this, I think the known components of our psychology as humans are wondrous because of how intricately they work together to develop our psyches as people. Whether you're talking individually or collectively, I'd argue we're very much composed by our genetics, social habits, religious ideas, subconscious biases, and of course technology as I just finished ranting about it. Most of that is common knowledge, but we often underestimate just how delicate our minds and perceptions are in the face of such factors day in and day out.

On a basic level, you have human emotion. I think it's worth noting that the way we feed or neglect to feed into them influences many of our biases we often ignore. What's more, emotions often manifest similar to shades on a color spectrum, with some being purer and others being more mixed and complex. That's something I've actually thought about more and more over the years as I've become more introspective in my own right. Honestly, I've learned I have a pretty complicated mind of my own, and one of the things I had to grapple with while growing up was convolution of my emotions and even sense of empathy at times. The contrast between such simple things as empathy and apathy I realized are far more nuanced than we often acknowledge in life. The latter generally encompasses a mindset of indifference, often resulting in what I'd label as dangerous detachment in some cases. The former however embracing sincere connection from interactions, yet also prone to blinding our better judgment as feelings can create bias. In reality, I think practicing a balance of the two is something we often overlook when going about even the most insignificant things in our daily lives. In the same way our raw emotions exist and blend on a spectrum, so too can our senses of empathy and apathy. On one hand it can create internal conflict over how we approach certain things, and on another people blindly use it to justify their personal perception. I'm even guilty of that myself.

On a deeper level, I don't think it's crazy to say that what we see in the world is often a reflection of what we see in ourselves. What we empathize or detach from in life, and how we think about this world in the way of morality, justice, spirituality, etc., it often originates from how we feel and think about our own identities. Funnily enough I actually realized this through a lot of arguments I've had with people. Often you'll find that when conflicts start becoming irrational, people will insult you in ways that make absolutely no sense, yet I'd argue part of that comes from people using their own insecurities and throwing them onto others at times. Personally, I've been on the receiving end of criticism only to think the other person is more so talking about *themselves* rather than me.

Don't get me wrong though, I'm not saying this is absolute, but rather that these perceptions we hold toward a given reality *partially* mirror the deepest parts of our psyches. Inversely, how we choose to look at the world also helps to develop our minds as we learn and grow over time. So, in short, our environments play on us just as much as we play on them. I think it's fairly easy to see how this is a fundamental way we engage with the world around us, yet I feel we as people often lack self-awareness of it in our own lives. Even when we do, we're often unwilling to analyze our own thinking on a deeper level introspectively. It's literally a matter of asking, "Why do I do the things that I do? Why do I feel certain things in these situations? Why does my rational thinking work the way it does? Why am I like this?" Now I'm just as guilty as the next guy scoffing at this some days from having the attitude of, "That's just the way I am, deal with it." Realistically, you just don't feel like being self-reflective every moment of your life when it can be so uncertain anyway. Regardless, I think one of the most important things I've learned in my time is the true necessity to be introspective as human beings. One way or another, you need to be able to examine the deepest, darkest depths of yourself, and just how you exist in the world around you. You have to be willing to contend with the various parts of your mind that may often be loud and overlap with each other.

Both in my own experience and observation, I've definitely found that easier said than done. I think a lot of people are hesitant to do this simply out of being uncomfortable from it. To volunteer to potentially upend your sense of identity is asking a lot for some, yet I'd still argue for the willingness to look at the best *and* worst parts of yourself going far below the surface. In my teen years, one of the ways I became accustomed to both thinking about and doing this basically came from giving myself frequent therapy sessions. It kind of calls from some imagination, but pretend for a moment that you're your own therapist, talking to yourself about any simple thought, feeling, or action you want to understand better in relation to who you are. Imagine this kind of dialogue as an example,

"I got mad and yelled at my friend today."

"Ok. Why?"

"They were annoying me"

"What were they doing that annoyed you?"

"They kept interrupting me while I was talking."

"Hm well they've always had a bad habit of doing that, but why does it bother you so much *now*?"

"I was venting, and I felt like I wasn't being heard."

"Is that something new you've been feeling lately?"

"Yeah"

"So does that explain your recent anger issues?"

"No, but it is part of the issue."

"What's another part of that?"

"I feel like people don't care about what I have to say about anything."

"Do you want people to care?"
"Yeah."
"Why?"
"I don't know."
"Do you think you're becoming more concerned with what others have to say about your input?"

You get the point. The aim is to keep going further and further down the rabbit hole of your own mind in order to better understand the root of your own psyche. This goes for the good, bad, strange, twisted, creative, spiritual, etc. To be honest though, it's really just a fancy, more productive way of talking to yourself. But hey, for someone like me who's probably spent more time of my life talking to myself than other people, that's not always a bad thing. See, I think you end up learning to think more unconventionally, from a multitude of angels you wouldn't expect to resonate with otherwise. In some cases, it takes more initiative and contemplation to give yourself such therapy than in the normal way people go through with a second person. It gives you a heightened sense of self awareness in comparison. When you're better able to look inward at your own basic psychology, along with the abnormal side of it, you're also able to dissect reality better when looking outward. Of course, such thinking isn't an outright *replacement* for conventional therapy, nor sure to make you see everything clearly in life. However, it does help reveal how much more sentient we are as people than we give ourselves credit for. From a biological perspective, we're all composed of mostly the same stuff, and subject to the same patterns of behavior marked as human nature. Yet to know how to shift and adapt one's psyche is an endeavor that's seen *tremendous* variance among humankind. It's that kind of uniqueness that gives us all a choice in manifesting what we envision in the world when it comes to ideas and different sentiments. Nurturing those modes of thinking and all the links between them is what drives us forward after all, although you have to acknowledge sometimes it's for the better and worst alike. At every twist and turn in history there've been people good at getting what they want by manipulating the thinking of others, whether it's for political power, financial advantages, heck, even the rise of cult leaders is a perfect example. The list goes on. By nature, it's impossible to completely mitigate that risk when you're talking about free thought or abstract ideas, but that's what makes the good ones more meaningful in my opinion. It's that sort of dual nature that allows us to shape the world in different directions.

Our minds are intricate states of being worth the same sentiment of wonder we attribute to the universe itself. Perhaps we often underestimate this, or maybe we just take it for granted. Despite how small we are in the grand scheme of the universe, the minuscule window of perception we're allowed shows us true uniqueness within our own humanity and the glimmers of life itself. How we think, as opposed to *what* we think, is one of the most important variables in seeing that for ourselves.

Making note of all that kind of segues into the matter of consciousness if we're *really* about going down rabbit holes. I mean, it kind of goes hand in hand with discussions about the human psyche right? Although, I will say it's probably worth examining how to *be* conscious about our place in the world before contemplating consciousness itself.

For one thing, my point about uniqueness found among us often makes me wonder about things like free will for instance. There's plenty of arguments that challenge my own feelings, asserting that such variety among our choices is a mere illusion when you acknowledge the ways human nature supersedes it. That, despite what we think we're in control of, we're not. To be fair, I do believe there's some validity to such ideas, or at the very least I can understand why people would hold such an existential viewpoint. When you really reflect on it, every thought you may feel is unique has been thought of by someone else, at some point within human history, even if it was never acted on. In theory, your thoughts, your perception, they're just repeats in the circle of life. There's nothing special about you or your worldview at all. The thing is, this is only true to a fine point. I kind of mean that literally to be honest.

See, I think that even as we evolve through millennia, so much of what we are as humans tend to repeat itself, albeit with slight variations, yet significant enough to influence the reality of our current existence. This kind of phenomena happens on a multitude of levels, with arguably the lowest being at the sole individual. When it comes to our own selves, so much of what we do, how we do it, and how we interpret it can be compared side by side with someone else in history. Of literally all the people that have existed at one point in time, it's likely that whatever experience, whatever sensation you may feel belongs to you, has also been felt by someone else at one moment or another. I think that's just *one* component connecting human beings together. It's this thing where, in a way, we indeed have a collectively shared consciousness, yet people neglect the small variations in who we are that keep such experiences from simply being carbon copies of each other. Obviously I'm very much talking from a philosophical standpoint here, but the basic concepts in genetics follow similar principles if we're being honest. In the same way genetic variance influences what makes you, *you,* so does our individual consciousness. There's a small percentage in that perception of reality that's never existed among any of the people that have come before you, and to tap into that perception, that state of unique clarity in your own right, is a journey in and of itself in life. At the risk of sounding anticlimactic, it all circles back to that sentiment of self-awareness.

It's not the most profound element of existence to contemplate, but it is one of the most *underrated* things to contemplate. In the context of one's psyche, we become aware of *who* we are, yet with consciousness, we become aware of *what* we are. It's getting as close to that root as possible in our endeavors that such simple thinking is the ultimate tool. Interestingly enough, I think few would dispute that such introspection on the *collective* level has always helped human beings study themselves, yet it's also caused a discrepancy between larger societies as a whole at times. In the same manner slight variation in one's identity sets them apart from others, so do the slight differences in group structures of people, except it often manifests in far more noticeable ways. For instance, you could have two countries that operate under what's essentially the same government, implement basically the same policy for something, yet the people of one will differ in attitude at their societal structure due to the wording of the policy on paper. From there it's easy to notice the various ripple effects caused by public opinion alone, influencing everything from their education system, healthcare, transportation, etc. Such minute, nuanced sentiments in people help make up layers of collective structures I'd say. You can go from countries to states to cities to towns to households, etc., each of these levels influenced by ripple effects in their own right, as well as different degrees of awareness toward why things play out within those systems in the manner they do. Ultimately, I think whether you're talking in a philosophical sense or even scientific sense, most takeaways from being self-aware of our realities yields the question of *why?* It's this universal question of true purpose in the presence of what we perceive to exist, very much an issue of contention both on the individual, and collective level for human beings.

Now, here's an anecdote for you. For a large part of my life, I used to live with an underlying idea that I really didn't belong anywhere or with anyone as a person. Don't get me wrong, I've always had friends and family I care for deeply, but for the most part, I was always pretty weird growing up (and still am honestly). It was never a secret that I was the black sheep of the family in many ways, and when it came to social interactions, being introverted has always been a part of who I am. Regardless, I always struggled to shake the idea that no matter how hard I'd try to find it, there would never really be any place or people I would truly belong to, that I would always be an outcast in some way no matter where I ended up in life.

If I'm being honest, this kind of insecurity isn't uncommon in kids or people in general, so I don't reflect on it as something unique to my life story at all. The significance is in what I learned from it as I got older. Having a sense of identity is deeply connected to having a sense of purpose, however it doesn't need to be rooted in one place or mindset the way some people think it does. The true nature of one's purpose isn't revealed as a single defining answer to explain the worth of your life. Rather, it manifests as a multitude of realities we play into on a daily basis. What I mean by this is, as you traverse through this world, and as you traverse through life in general, the small roles we play in each other's lives and personal stories have far greater impact on a daily basis than we're often aware of. In that way, you have a purpose to serve everywhere you find yourself, even when that sentiment *feels* absent and intangible. Again, I realize that sounds a bit simplistic in a way, especially if you really are someone who feels lost in life, but being aware you hold such influence over reality is one step closer to embracing it in a way that ails the existential dread you might feel at the moment. Even the seemingly insignificant small talk with the cashier at a fast-food place might brighten their day in a way that sticks with them moving forward.

Looking at it from a larger perspective, I really do feel this is a small part of how people find each other when crossing paths in life. It's astonishing that our lives can intersect with one another through even the most seemingly *minute* actions we take. When we're conscious of this kind of influence, it becomes easier to understand that even the slightest awareness of who *and* what you are can either elevate, or deteriorate your existence in a way that affects everything around you.

What we start being conscious of originates in ourselves and extends outward in our broader communities. The benefit of realizing this makes us less likely to become stuck in fixed molds of thinking as we play out our roles in collective society. If we're to marvel at how small we are in the grand scheme of the universe, then it's also our responsibility to note the value of everyone's imprint on it. At the end of the day, I truly believe our human potential on all levels will always be intertwined in those markings.

Pain and suffering is a natural part in seeing the grace of life

In life, pain exists as a driving force behind many human endeavors, good and bad. We all experience it at one point or another. Maybe it's physical, mental, or emotional, but regardless of what kind, part of being human is enduring pain. Part of *living* on the other hand, is growing from it.

To be honest, there's quite a bit of overlap with the different kinds of adversity we face in life. On one level, mental and emotional pain is what we most resonate with at an early stage in life. I mean, think about it, people often underestimate just how *delicate* and impressionable a child's mind is early on. As bleak as it sounds, it's pretty easy to traumatize a kid in such a way that haunts them for years to come. A lot of times, the dysfunction we're exposed to in the world leaves at least *some* mark on us moving forward. There's no such thing as a human being that's not damaged in some way. It's natural after all. We're delicate beings drifting through the universe by default.

As a whole, we're innately prone to things like, regret, fear, loss, loneliness, heartbreak, hate, rage, etc. At the root of it all is just hurt though. Nobody *wants* to hurt, but everyone does. If there's one thing I've learned however, it's that you'll find some don't handle it well, and others seek to rid themselves of pain and suffering entirely, which is a hollow pursuit in the long run.

In terms of the former, you'll sometimes see damaged people going through the motions of everyday life without actively trying to make things better for themselves. Some become so familiar with all the suffering and trauma in their lives that it's all they know. It's all they've grown to recognize. They live in a state where they can't even imagine being able to heal and move forward. Addicts for example, regardless of substance, or just people whose lifestyle has clearly deteriorated.

On the latter front, there are those willing to do whatever it takes to either cope or be rid of the angst that ails them, and the means to that end are vast to say the least. It could range from a parent burying themselves in work to distract from the death of their child, or just pushing away those they love the most, all the way to someone getting off on hurting others. It's a dark and hollow pursuit ultimately, yet I feel we all do this subconsciously at some point in our lives, especially when you consider how rarely people choose to directly deal with some of the darker, more traumatizing things they've faced in life. It's an interesting phenomena really, because in doing this, we become more and more damaged as we try to sidestep our issues, ultimately ending up in that state of emptiness, unable to see the potential for anything beyond it.

Understand however, that's only a small yet highly significant part of how we perceive pain through our mental and emotional lenses. On a deeper level, there are those who end up traveling down a much darker path partially because of what they've gone through. Pain is just one of the *many* essences of life with the power to corrupt one's soul to the point of no return. Don't get me wrong now, I believe there are plenty of flat out evil individuals in the world who have always indulged in disturbingly malicious lifestyles. Those whose nature is embedded in what can only be described as true darkness. That's just how some humans are unfortunately. Despite this, there are people who, in their heart of hearts are decent, yet still lose their way in life. People who develop a twisted philosophy/perception on life and the world, and it starts to affect how they treat themselves, as well as those around them.

In the grand scheme of things however, to be presented with such adversity capable of truly breaking you is a necessary part of our human existence. To some extent, you don't know who you really are until you've had to face true hurt inside yourself. Until you've had to make a choice at what to do when it's staring you in the face. Until you've been forced to figure out how to move forward in a healthy way, in spite of whatever circumstances you're dealing with. All while acknowledging the most tempting coping mechanisms our world tends to offer.

Those same trials and tribulations also test us physically on the flip side. Although, you gotta admit, it isn't *really* the flip side when you consider how interconnected the mind and body are. In both senses humans are severely vulnerable to so much of what exists in our world and the universe. Even compared to other species on earth, we're all pretty frail organisms. Things like sports and competition are probably the most obvious and visual examples to show how we temper that frailness into something greater. Running, combat sports, using the laws of physics and projectiles to create games like basketball, football, tennis, heck even pool; they all show us how growth is possible in the confines of the human condition. Sometimes you'll see athletes that harness more of their physicality than anything else, and vice versa with competitors that rely on strategy and skill built on repetition. In either practice the essence of one's being is only malleable through the struggles we endure, not in the absence of them. I think this truly applies to everyone, regardless of physical ability, mental capacities, or class.

We live in a complex world, one not everybody traverses on equal footing. Some of us live in bigger houses or have more money. Some have greater influence or opportunity as public figures and personalities than others. Some of us are born short and will never be that good in a game of basketball, while others are genetically gifted freaks that dominate any sport they play. The fact of the matter is, if you pick any day to go outside and just observe the world around you for a few hours or so, no matter how you slice it, you'll see many of us live on different levels in terms of lifestyle and the problems we run into. And yet, regardless of circumstance over a lifetime, sooner or later we're all tested. Sooner or later we're all challenged with something that threatens everything we are as not just humans, but as *people*, and even the most comfortable lifestyle won't give the answers on how to overcome them.

In general, pain gives us just the *slightest* peek into the vastness of the darkest life essences. Things like fear, anger, regret, sadness, loneliness, resentment, etc., they're all capable of morphing not just who we are and how we view reality, but even deteriorate our overall health as a whole, mentally and physically. At the same time though, it offers us an opportunity to refine everything we are as human beings. Individually, we find healthy ways to cope and grow from our experiences, and collectively, we're given a choice to build up others we can empathize with along the way. Don't get me wrong now, it doesn't always go smoothly, but consider this; so much artistic inspiration in societies around the world have roots in despair and the lessons learned from it. Honestly, I'd argue music and comedy are two of the *best examples.* I mean, too many genres and senses of humor to list have contemplated the essence of pain and suffering for *literal centuries.* The same goes for other creative expressions like paintings, drawings, sculptures, books, movies, etc. They often offer these shared ideas and feelings of angst, but also ways to rise above them. They inspire us to do and be more when the need arises. That being said, I think it's fair to say humanity often proves to have more potential than fragility at times.

In many ways, the nature of suffering is the precursor to experiencing grace in this life. I think that's why it's important to be thankful for the times we truly *are* at peace with ourselves and life around us. Those moments end up being the ultimate payoff through everything we endure really, no matter how dark or bleak. Oddly enough, they're not guaranteed to any of us in this lifetime, but that's only another reason we have to never give up on finding them, nor to ever give up on ourselves or each other. By the end of it all, pain inevitably changes all of us, but whether it's for the better or worse is something we all decide for ourselves. That's not just staying alive, that's living.

The world isn't black and white

Very often, I think we forget just how subjective one's individual worldview is. There are so many elements to perceiving the world we live in, whether they be genetics, environment, or our raw experiences. At one point or another in life, you learn the difference between right and wrong, good and evil; it's not as clear cut as we're taught as children.

So many issues we often contemplate and debate hold far more complexity than we could possibly imagine. Something controversial like taking a life is a perfect example to start out with. To assert the argument that it's absolutely *never* acceptable to take another life is just as absurd as saying it's *always* acceptable. People like police officers and military personnel are forced to deal with that reality all the time. The point being, such an issue is far too complicated to have an *absolute* opinion on. When it comes to issues related to how we govern ourselves, whether we're talking lawfully, politically, spiritually, etc., I think it's pretty dangerous to look at them as black and white. When people start basing their actions around absolute perspectives, it leads to chaos. Eventually it always results in one's downfall. It's pretty easy to see this in society actually. I mean, just look at how more people are engaging in politics within the last few decades. In an age where public discourse is at its most active, to say discussion of certain topics has become toxic and closed minded is very much an understatement. In today's era of new thinking it's much easier to see how we place other positions and ideas in boxes, often to our own detriment. Don't get me wrong though, sometimes categorizing people, ideas and policies is actually needed. Looking at things as either Democrat or Republican, left or right, liberal or conservative, does admittedly aid in labeling where people stand on certain things in a *general* sense. But after all the time we've spent drawing and moving those lines in the sand through history, I personally think the way we've grown to embrace them is kinda, well, dumb, in the grand scheme of things. Trust me, as boring as it can be sometimes, politics is an inherent element to any sustainable civilization. Objectively speaking, you literally need it to help establish order among sentient life. It's when Your perspective willingly ignores so much of the other realities persisting in our world that we just come off as pretty...ignorant, to say the least.

At the same time, this problem has been long standing in religious culture as well. Now, I'm religious myself, and happen to be a fairly spiritual person in general. Yet I've also been in too many spaces with people who treat certain sets of teachings as the *only* values worth adhering to. It's sort of this hive mindset that's really *always* been perpetuated through different circles in history. Even the best people at heart have been guilty of close mindedness. One's religion becomes the embodiment of their identity, and everything they experience is filtered through a set spiritual template. What makes it worse is anything that challenges that mindset is labeled as dangerous opposition. The word "heathenish" comes to mind in describing them. Maybe it's obvious, but the same phenomena applies not just to religion, nor politics, but really any group structure people can get carried away with, all the way to sports teams or even television fandoms for crying out loud. I guess it's easier to make sense of the world like that. Most people can accept there will always be things beyond our understanding as humans, but it's the pursuit of widening the *scope* of that understanding, that, while typically burdened with risk, is usually the most rewarding. In reality, it really comes down to whether we're oppressing a wider range of thought capable of connecting us rather than dividing us. I know it sounds basic, but we all have a tendency to reject such open mindedness. Human beings are stubborn after all, there's no denying that, and we're usually slow to rearrange our worldview even if the world calls for it.

Fact of the matter is, if there's even a hint of validity found in differing ideas, then they're still worth a conversation. On the other hand, it's important to be rooted in your own convictions in trying to hear everyone out. I've seen plenty of people that willingly adjust their opinion or perspective to fit the attitudes of whatever environment or people they're around. In a sense, some of us are more impressionable than others, but without thinking for yourself, you may end up conforming to ideals you're incompatible with.

In the simplest of explanations, it's the acknowledgement of different realities that begins to foster human potential. Those ideas are one of the many things driving us to take action in our lives. How we *embrace* them however influences the *quality* of those actions, as well as the succeeding interactions with the world. I think people fail to see this for a number of reasons, but one of the most detrimental ones being that we seldom encourage critical thinking among ourselves or society, or if we do, it's sometimes superficial. Often in the service of things like manipulative rhetoric or agendas. For some people and circles it's easier to simply push more *rigid*, specific ways in which to think, or even *what* to think period than to risk deeper thought that might not align with everything they see in the world.

That being said, it's worth pointing out there's nothing wrong in not empathizing with every possible perspective or reality to the degree others might. Like I alluded to earlier, for as deep as the inner workings of people, the planet we live on, and the universe we live in may be, even the most enlightened of us can't explore all of it. As a species, we're not designed to connect with everything on every level. You'll see things and meet people with experiences you'll never empathize with 100%, but that's to be expected. It's the awareness of alternate realities and truths that reinforce just how complicated our world truly is. In that sense, I'd say there are few *absolute* truths to how we exist, but rather universal ones we're all subject and can relate to. Human themes that have stood the test of time throughout our existence, and will probably continue to do so, regardless of whatever advancements we make, albeit expressed with variation of course. Cautionary tales of human flaws like greed, lust, arrogance take on many forms throughout history, as do tales of love, friendship, innovation, and fulfillment. In times of both achievement and tragedy, they manage to make themselves known.

Together they blend to form molds for us to fall into from time to time. Whether that's being tempted to act on our most childish emotions, or feeling nervous at rolling the dice on something that could change your life, we all get caught up in the varying mores of being human, coming from all sides and angles. They're the things that influence all of us, regardless of where you land on a political or religious spectrum. They're the things that, even in an artificial age of existence and interaction, will play their hand on whatever human beings are meant to become someday. Tyrants can be made even among the people that are supposed to be the "morally right," or "good guys." War on the smallest scale of even an online community can birth and become something toxic if people are left to their darkest devices. Likewise, the potential for life to meaningfully connect and build with other life is always fulfilled in some capacity sooner or later. That's the kicker really, the one absolute I can safely advocate is life always finds a way to persist past what binds it.

By nature, our world and universe have a tendency to unravel new elements that rattle our understanding of it, regardless of one's grip on any given subject. At the same time, don't just simply subscribe to whatever new information you run into without dissecting it. Have ideas that are your own, and look to refine them through different learning experiences you find yourself in. In trying to map where those experiences intersect, we start to understand the realities we partake in without even realizing it.

Hope & Faith

Okay, so Hope and faith are these weird essences that are quite literally intangible. Like, it's common knowledge we can track where chemicals coding for things such as love, fear, ethics, morals, even just plain optimism, are all located in the brain. Yet when you look at how our species has embraced such things as hope and faith, both in a secular and religious fashion, it's just not something numerically traceable in any way, (although you could make the argument that they're more present as a combination of neural process in our minds, but I digress). The point is, the essence of both concepts are abstract in nature, yet simultaneously inherent in how we live our lives. Traditionally we view them as ailments to aid in adversity, and, well, that's because they always have been. They're the precursors to the smallest forms of optimism when you really think about it, and I think few would argue they transcend being human. Even though we don't always acknowledge it, I feel most people already realize how much these essences permeate *all* life. Even in interacting with other species like our pets and animals that encompass different ecosystems, we hold hope that the communication barriers don't hold us back from coexisting peacefully. We have faith that the steps we take to ensure that are worth it. In the midst of life's most uncertain variables, hope, and faith are what keep us tethered to our humanity. They're what help reveal our "why" for living.

I should probably be clear though. For one thing, being hopeful or having faith isn't *exclusive* to adversity or dark times in life, in many ways we engage with such ideas even in our happiest, most stable moments. During the times when everything is going well and we have what we want also sees us ask for more out of life, or at the very least, ask for the knowledge on how to sustain it. Likewise, we rely on the potential of the human spirit, and for some of us, a higher power beyond it to guide us through harsher times. The thing is, I feel we *sometimes* miss the point when it comes to embracing either sentiment. Take hope specifically, and I'd argue we don't always accept it into our lives as best we could per se. That's not to say there's a *definitive way* to view it, but consider this; there are infinite things that exist in the entirety of planet earth *and* the universe itself that can easily reduce human beings to *nothing*. Things easily capable of reducing us down to our lowest level, if not break us completely, and I say this in all senses you could possibly think of, i.e. physically, emotionally, spiritually, psychologically, etc. We sometimes underestimate this reality until we're thrust into the middle of it. That goes for our bright moments too, as they can hurt us when we get too comfortable and stagnate. In the face of such challenges, something like hope is rarely enough to survive or grow from them. In essence, hope is a driving force for humans to have control over their fate, even when probability is stacked against them. To have hope is to have a call to action you're relentless in pursuing based on what you can do to make a situation better. Even if all you *can* do to make things better, or someone else's situation better is changing your attitude, that has immense impact on the betterment of everyone. By nature we feed off the energy, mindsets, and perspectives of one another without even realizing it. Even in the most non communicative ways we're all able to influence the morale of an environment, either bringing it up or down. The succeeding step in that process is actually *acting* on that newfound motivation. What's the use of being optimistic if you're not actively building on what can be improved in this world? In the same way life often puts us through the ringer to test us, it also asks us to step up in such moments that require hope, rather than waste them on wishful thinking.

Faith serves as a counterpart to this I feel. The two go hand in hand when you think about it, and you could probably argue in some cases it's even *more* necessary, spiritual or otherwise. It envelops hope really. In its simplest form, faith is the trust that all we put into the basic act of living on this rock has a payoff. If human beings can derive motivation and give life to their greatest hopes, then the actual journey of doing so requires confidence that it actually *means* something. That it's worth it. Obviously we all express and observe this in various ways, and that's probably one of the best things about it honestly. The essence of both hope and faith is so malleable that rarely is it ever fully confined in human history. Even in the most rigid of settings, they're tied to creativity and visions of the future by even the most ordinary people. All the confidence in the world doesn't guarantee that things will work out in the long run. Many times, they don't. But then again, *most* of the time, our success stories don't play out exactly as we picture either. We're constantly reminded that even through the variables we'll never have control over, there are so many paths to transcending our limitations as people.

What's scary, at least to me, is knowing how easily we can forget this at times, although I'll admit it's perfectly human to do so. No one is motivated 24/7 nor do we always feel like all our burdens will pay off and make us better someday. It's normal to read everything I just wrote and still feel a bit 'meh' about our endeavors some days. But what I've learned is sometimes remembering or feeling such belief, however it's expressed, comes as fragments in life. They're revelations revealed in moments we experience and hold onto. Moments that give meaning to everything we may ponder over in terms of life and still unanswered questions. Personally, I've found the best ones usually come unexpectedly. Not always when you want them, but they're there, often in the midst of chaos, strife, or even benign uncertainty. Even if it's not in a straight line, they guide us forward, just a little bit at least, offering a hint of clarity. Being able to see and appreciate that, not only in your own life, but in the lives of others is useful. If you can help someone else heed them, you're also helping yourself in reality. It sounds basic but the mutual commitment to lift other people up is one of the *many* things that prevent life from stagnating. To abandon that is to do the opposite. A world where no one attempts to pass along hope or faith isn't dark solely in the sense of doom and gloom, but also dark in the way of hollow human spirits. Sure, everything shallow and superficial about ourselves and the societies we create might persist regardless, but what's the point if there's not even a *chance* in fostering substance to them in the long run? To me, such a reality is fragile beyond belief.

At this point, I'm sure almost everyone has heard the phrase "where there's life there's hope." That's true, but honestly, I also believe they're one and the same. The presence of life itself is an embodiment of hope. Life in this universe, whether exclusive to earth or not, whether randomized or spawned from a god or not, is proof of the inherent beauty in creation, persisting through everything we know and don't know. To see and embrace that in ourselves, how it connects between each other, *as well* as how it's not exclusive to humans makes all the difference, even when it doesn't seem like it some days. It allows us to act in spite of those mundane or dispassionate feelings. Our faith in light of uncertainty however *is* what makes us uniquely human. Even the most rational endeavors of science that seek to understand everything are mired in some faith. Faith that what we derive from observations, research and experiments will benefit the world despite all the things that can and will inevitably go wrong, i.e., scientific misconduct, political corruption, etc. In light of that, we still push forward to literally optimize our existence as a species, no matter how fraught it seems at times. Ultimately, it's comical how quick we are to categorize these concepts as merely religious or spiritual, when they run much deeper in terms of who and what we are in this world. In the end I can only hope more people understand that as time goes on.

Imagination-something this title lacks

You know, I think another significant aspect of our identity as people lies in how we utilize our imaginations across time and space. On the surface that idea sounds simple enough I admit. I mean, imagination is practically a *fundamental* ingredient for creativity and innovation when you think about it. That's the thing oddly enough. To even arrive at a sense of imagination requires some form of *thinking itself* paired with *feeling* I'd argue. I know that notion sounds a bit rigid, but hear me out. True imagination combines thinking with feeling, any feeling, into a sort of mental flow state. A flow state that's constantly reinvented through millennia across generations I might add.

See, by now we all realize that as times change, so do people, places, and the world itself as it's known to human beings. Between all the countless wars, revolutions, discoveries, breakthroughs, social movements, etc., our world has switched trajectory time and time again while still moving forward in the name of human progress. Part of that comes from people across history who dared to reinvent their own thinking. I don't even mean anything too major by that really. Just regular people that would process life differently on a day to day basis and grew from it. People that ended up producing the most interesting parts of human culture and innovation, like music, comedy, television, fictional stories, etc. I've said before that music and comedy are two examples of artistic expression rooted in despair in some instances. I still find that to be true, but it's also worth pointing out how *both* are capable of manipulating individual *and* collective realities. Music, simply put, can evoke emotion, change the tone of an atmosphere—even physical feelings and memories can interact with the *infinite* compositions of sound waves we create. It's hard not to be fascinated at how varying lyrical compositions, presentation, etc., can shed clarity on how you're feeling, or even encompass a mood you've lived with for years now. Inversely the same can be said for a *lack thereof.* Silence is just as impactful depending on how it's used in stories or entertainment. Think about how many times you've felt a sense of suspense toward a fight in an action movie because of the soundtrack, and likewise, how a *lack* of soundtrack in say, a horror film, can also create suspense. Or better example, think of how music can amp up your motivation to do a tough workout. I think plenty of people reading this can attest that once you get fired up by an energetic track, you go harder in whatever you're doing than if you didn't. The point is, in nature sounds are rebranded and reimagined all the time. Sometimes it's through songs that influence culture, and other times they're just small melodies paired with random activities or environments. Something as simple as birds chirping in a park can exude genuine tranquility that may resonate with someone for instance. Being able to truly *listen* to such things gives insight on the many levels of creative essence we interact with audibly. At the end of the day they're all different vibes with their own energy for us to build relationships with. Like, haven't you ever stumbled across a song that perfectly encapsulates how you were feeling around the time you found it? That's partly the reason I don't have a favorite genre of music (much to people's annoyance when they ask). I grew up connecting with everything from The Temptations and Earth, Wind, and Fire, all the way to anime openings and video game soundtracks. More often than not I found at least *some* kind of inspiration in different melodies from all walks of life, and from different eras at that. You'd be surprised how conveniently the human experience is captured in sound to put it bluntly.

Comedy is the same way in a sense. It has many layers that shift places in terms of what's relevant in society I'd say. laughter may be the best medicine, but what constitutes as funny or humorous is obviously subjective, yet also a major point of contention in modern day. Still, the fact that *so many* different senses of humor exist shows how multi-dimensional human thinking has become. Memes are a perfect example for Christ sake! To say they permeate culture is a *vast* understatement, especially considering how memes have become a culture unto itself. The thing is, despite *all* the ways you could define them, memes are pretty sophisticated humor made simple for everyone to enjoy. The wild card in this is how relevant or *irrelevant* some memes can be based on popularity, and honestly, that usually affects how funny people view them. It also opens the door for a new kind of meta humor when people reference old, played out memes inside of fresh ones, where the joke is sometimes a reference to how people responded to a meme in the past. Basically tiers of memes that build off each other in addition to internet culture as a whole.

What's funny is there's gotta be at least someone that doesn't know what I'm talking about. Or at least someone cringing at the fact that I just tried to explain memes unironically. The fact of the matter is comedic culture has evolved to where brands of humor branch out so fervently that the self-awareness *alone* is funny. Although of course, people still argue over which jokes are, but that's neither here nor there. Either way I still have too many memes on my phone (and people who know me personally can vouch for this) but I digress.

Of course, there's always more conventional art forms people resonate with. Things like drawing, painting, sketching, and also things like dance for instance. I for one...cannot dance, *but* I was pretty good at drawing back in the day. I went through middle school filling out notebooks with doodles and amateur comics about tons of different fantasy ideas. As you can imagine I took inspiration from a myriad of styles to create my own (although I gotta concede they were a far cry from being impressive compared to other works I've seen). Nevertheless, that free reign of creativity is essential as water for people to thrive as opposed to just surviving. It's the ability to experiment with different art forms and the innovation that goes into all of them. To put it bluntly, that's what adds spice to this life. When you take people focused enough to think critically about their craft, and see how they combine it with their passion, those are the ones able to push the boundaries of their imagination. The ones who turn their *best* ideas into their *worst* ones because they keep surpassing them.

Pardon the left turn, but to be honest, it'd probably be irresponsible to exclude something like sports from that description, despite what I think is a general consensus that sports is the *opposite* of "art," but I disagree. I played about as much of them as a kid as I drew comics and played Nintendo. It just took me well into my later years to appreciate what they exude in the way of innovative craft. It's no secret that competition, in any space, can breed toxicity and be destructive, but when it's balanced with respect and maturity for one's opponent(s), it's capable of motivating everyone involved. I think when you experience firsthand how hard someone is willing to go and compete against your best self, and what they *channel* to do so, it's telling of their character to some extent, not merely as an athlete or competitor but also as a person seeking greatness in many regards. Some train, fight or compete for money, legacy, culture, or even just for the sake of tapping into a survival mindset. Yet regardless of motivation or sport, the successful athletes always combine a sense of strategic thought with instinctive skill. It's reaching that zone that allows you to put your own unique expression on it. A sort of flow state if you will. That kind of focus on one's craft extends to so many more areas than we would think requires extensive imagination.

To be frank though, plenty of us get a big head about what truly defines something as art or imaginative at times. We'll put somewhat rigid definitions around what they should specifically encapsule, yet much of it is constantly reinvented in both essence *and* manifestation through generations. Trust me, I've heard a lot of hot takes explaining why certain kinds of art *"Isn't really art,"* because it supposedly lacks a certain element. Or why certain types of film and entertainment *need* to be represented and consumed a certain way in order to have meaning. I'm even guilty of it in my own right honestly. I've listened to plenty of newly released music and chalked it up to straight trash...some of which I still stand by, but that's not the point. The point is, it's still music, even if it doesn't personally resonate with *my* taste. By nature these crafts we so passionately engage in are *meant* to change and be reinvented as time goes on and on. They go through stages of being groundbreaking, to becoming mainstream, and finally on the way out as outdated. In essence creativity without such fluidity is anything but.

Now, despite so many of our ideas often repeating, or "rhyming," as Mark Twain would put it, I think every generation holds the capacity to make their mental state formless in the grand scheme of things. Part of that means learning to adapt and shift one's creative process in as many ways as possible. That's why I bring up so many different things we pour our souls into as people. The universal presence of such a flow state can be found among *any* craft really. It's just a matter of cross study if you want to broaden what you specialize in yourself. When you can be formless in such a manner unique to your own progression, thinking critically about the link between so many disciplines becomes easier. In turn, it *also* becomes easier to surpass a lot of the limits people will place on creative expression. People in every generation find different ways to manifest this, albeit it's not the case for *everybody*. As harsh as it sounds, there will always be people that just don't focus that into their own being. Not because they're incapable or inferior, but rather we often get distracted by things that don't *truly* aid in becoming our best selves to say the least. In some ways we're all guilty of indulging in trivial or shallow content spewed out by our societies. The thing is, some people never find something beyond it in their lifetime.

Ironically, those distractions can come from the *very* sources and art forms I've talked about when there's little to no substance to them. See, there's inherently a dual nature to all of this. Too much of any one thing and it becomes oversaturated and diluted at the same time. Likewise, too *little* exposure to the finer things in life and you could very well witness people whose imaginations are repressed and stifled. Everything in between is what we traverse on a daily basis. Trying to find the right balance of thinking with feeling and turning the expression that follows into something *meaningful*. Something *fun* even.

At the end of the day, balance by nature is ever fleeting. There's always something around the corner to take us off it, to disrupt our focus. That's one of the fundamental challenges of being human after all. We're innately tasked with finding meaning in life beyond basic survival, beyond merely escaping the myriad of things in the universe that could easily kill us. That's why I think it's fair to say such fluid creativity is akin to a thread actually. A delicate thread woven among many facets of life through millennia. How that thread connects people together through creativity is always changing, both collectively and individually. It just takes a formless mind to notice it.

Let's talk about love and relationships, shall we?

Ok so there's *a lot* to unpack when it comes to contemplating love. These days when you bring up the subject, people show exhaustion at the constant mention of what's deemed hippie talk about loving everyone, peace amongst all, togetherness, that sort of thing. Admittedly I've been one of these people at different points, but simple empathy is, without question, an integral part of how we traverse this planet as sentient beings, so why wouldn't you at least try to make sense of the thing that's traditionally known for not making sense at all?

For one thing, it's important to realize that the perception on how to generally define love, romantic or platonic, differs on a much deeper scale amongst human beings. Obviously there's a plethora of cultural interpretations, from the idea that love is a part of the heart and soul to the idea that it doesn't exist past a chemical reaction in the brain. Likewise exist different perspectives on what certain relationship dynamics should be not only among different people, but among sentient life in general, i.e. animals, pets, nature, etc. For humans, there are all sorts of reasons why we come into one another's lives, and all sorts of reasons why people stay a part of them. Some are good, others are bad. In my own experience, I can honestly say every single person I've had a meaningful relationship with has entered my life in a weird or unexpected way. But that's the thing about finding people in life, the most significant ones are usually those you never asked to be in it.

There are endless dynamics to describe how we connect with each other, but getting straight to the meat and potatoes, you'd probably think of romantic relationships first right? I mean, it *is* how the human race has procreated across every homo species after all. It's no secret we tend to put the idea of being *with* someone in different stages or levels based on affinity links. I.e. flirting, just talking to gauge their personality, *casually* dating, *serious* dating, etc. Generally speaking, those levels can be rearranged for a *plethora* of reasons among the varied people in our world. For instance, someone like myself can't really commit to someone physically without feeling connected with them emotionally and mentally first, but interestingly enough, there are plenty of people who are the exact *opposite*. There are people who kind of *need* a sort of physical compatibility as a prerequisite before connecting emotionally. Personality types, traits, preferences, they all play a role in how we perceive both ourselves and the people we engage with. They play a role in the *simplest* ways we connect without us even realizing it.

Like I've said, our modes of communication have increased exponentially beyond what anyone imagined over the last half century. One consequence is more people than ever living introspectively while also understanding the complexities and intricacies of psychology. Even the most ordinary person could probably cite daddy issues or maybe childhood traumas as a reason for trust issues later in life if I'm being frank. That kind of reflection (while sometimes awkward depending on when it's brought up in conversation) is far less taboo today than a few decades ago. People are more willing to admit that these things not only affect them, but that we're capable of leaving each other with different kinds of imprints that potentially last a lifetime. A big part of this deals with a more *digital* ability to communicate, especially in the case of romance. Whether we're conscious of it or not, I think many of us influence our partners through digital means much more profoundly than we give ourselves credit for. I mean, the simplest example any of you reading this could relate to are texting exchanges right? If you believe someone to message you in a *particular* way exclusive to them, you may get anxiety over something as small as a longer window between replies for instance. That causes paranoia for some people that maybe their other is upset at them for something, or maybe something was said out of bounds. Or perhaps you read something and feel like their tone of voice just changed over text because they used a period, or even a lack of emojis depending on the person. This all sounds pretty miniscule compared to some of the more *legitimate* problems keeping us up at night right? But you know as well as I do that many people from teenagers to grown adults hold these worries when it comes to things like messaging in *any* capacity. Before you know it, you have two people arguing over made up scenarios that either don't exist or really aren't that big of a deal. The same thing goes for social media posts, commenting, sharing, or just *any* way you could share your digital footprint with someone else. Now of course this applies to platonic relationships too, but in the context of romance, the manner we give power to these different scenarios and outcomes is *especially* powerful. Without even realizing it, we interact with these mental simulations of how someone we care for might be feeling or acting in relation to ourselves or something else, and we act on those projections more often than not. We simulate the deeper meanings of those relationships and the direction they're taking all the time. The good thing is this isn't to make it seem like we're these mentally unstable creatures by nature. Honestly, I think we also do this in a good way as well. Sometimes we imagine the *best*-case scenario to play out among each other and, well, it creates some positive energy we could all use every now and then. That's the kicker actually. Human beings have always been capable of manipulating each other on many levels, both for the better and worse. But in today's day and age, that reach has extended much further than anyone's been able to measure thus far. Again though, that's not something to automatically fear per se, but it is worth taking note over.

The ripple effects can be seen on many levels, but on one of them, I think it's fair to say we've grown far more eccentric when it comes to love in recent times. I say that because in reality, love, depictions of romance, marriage, they've kind of *always* been misrepresented as overly whimsical if we're being honest with ourselves. I mean just go read some works written by century old poets...a lot of those guys just wanted to get laid at the end of the day. That's still the case today, but I think people still view love as this grandiose thing that can *always* work miracles and *always* provide fulfillment if you're willing to fight for it and give your all. The thing is, a lot of those arguments are pretty valid, just *not* to the degree people make them out to be. I know I sound like I'm complaining, but we tend to act like there's some sort of finish line to finding sustainable romance, or as if there's a fine point we just need to endure and hold out 'till. Then things will be easier, you'll be happier, etc., etc. Picture every stereotypical romance film you can think of, and it's easy to see how those plot lines are presented as the highest ideal to reach for in life. Don't get me wrong though, that's obviously not the *intention* of *every* writer or filmmaker but you get the point. We're more in love with the *idea* of that sentiment, the *idea* of the happy ending, the *idea* of what someone could be in our life...than what actually goes into a relationship itself. Simply put, plenty of people will overcommit in giving all of themselves to someone because of that.

What ends up happening is many relationships burn themselves out like a flame. They become artificial when giving yourself to someone is only to fill in a preconceived picture of fulfillment in our heads. Ironically you see that with selfless and selfish people alike. Across that spectrum are all sorts of people where, even when their vision for happiness is relatable, it isn't very flexible.

Think of it like running a race for instance. Regardless of the distance, many people get hyped and motivated to go all out from the very beginning, and, for a while, they go far, but sooner or later, they burn out, having only but so much of themselves to exert. That goes for anything from 400 meters to a marathon. Even if you finish the race, it becomes a much longer, and often painful process to see through to the end. When you have nothing left to give, every step forward is done on autopilot, because, well, it's better than stopping right? Moral of the story is, whether you're running alone or alongside someone in life, you need to pace yourself. Most people, even the ones who finish pretty well don't. We're constantly told that life is short, and to give it our all for someone we love in the most passionate way. That's partially true, but despite how short life can be, *living* is also the longest thing you'll ever be a part of. Take your time and grow into someone that you're proud of while also taking steps with someone at a carefully growing pace, because at the end of the day, if you're not satisfied with the person in the mirror, if you can't love yourself, how can you expect someone else to? A relationship that's truly healthy will see two people making each other better as a result of this. Not for the sake of repealing each other's flaws, but rather to extend what light and faith that's already present to places you never thought possible, one small step at a time. I think that's the best of yourself you can truly give someone.

Of course, people structure their relationships in so many other ways than just that, and in reality you could argue the pros and cons to all of them within the world today. But ultimately, that sentiment of learning what it means to share the best of yourself with other people is an important root element. Romantic or otherwise, even the greatest of us, with all our noble intentions are capable of the most damaging kinds of indifference, hate and toxicity when we're not careful. But that's the key word however, "*capable*." By nature humans are capable of the worst kinds of atrocities when they flat out don't care, or are motivated by darkness or twisted ideologies without even realizing it. To love each other and life Itself isn't an antidote to *any* of that. It's accepting how present all the disturbing things in this world are, yet choosing to nurture the best out of all life. *All* relationships are inherently *beyond* hard to sustain indefinitely. Friendships, ties to your parents, polygamous ties, even business and professional relationships (honestly you could probably change that to be *especially* hard, let's be honest). They all go through different phases as we grow and change as people. How you give the best of yourself to *anyone* is yet another thing that's tested through those stages in life. It's a test in what we choose to cultivate together as such a fragile species, undeniably connected in ways we rarely pay attention to. When we do though, I honestly believe we're reminded and motivated by why it's worth pursuing.

No one is empathetic every moment of every single day, and in reality you probably shouldn't be despite what I've said about things like hate and indifference. The truth is those essences are needed to understand the *conscious choice* to love, to just be kind. As harsh as it may sound, it takes more to be the one who's self-aware of their own toxicity, yet choose to be better for the sake of everyone impacted by your existence, from strangers in Starbucks to your family at home. It's harder to truly *be* that than the character who's morally virtuous through the whole story, but in the end it's also worth more. That kindness is priceless. When you commit to it, that kindness permeates every relationship you have, on every level, and someday you may just leave the world a *tad* bit better than how you found it. Thing is it's pretty hard, and it'll probably result in heartbreak in more ways than you could imagine. Most of the people you meet and interact with *will* leave your life sooner or later, and while you could definitely play devil's advocate to that statement, even the best-case goodbyes can hurt. Just missing a friend you can't talk to weighs on you without question. Likewise you'll meet people who, despite your genuine feelings, treat you like trash. Like I said earlier, we're pretty good at manipulating one another, and unfortunately plenty of people take no issue doing that to others trying to reach out to them, physically or mentally. And yet, for the people still motivated to connect with others even through that despair, well, they're ahead of the curve in a lot of ways. It's all about at least *trying* to have those relationships be defined by something that lasts even if you don't.

When it comes to this idea of loving everybody, being kind and being nice are two *very* different things. Everyone knows how to be nice, but a lot fewer are kind. To give the best of yourself to someone or even just the world in general is sometimes thankless. Some days you put in more than your loved one because that's just the way it is for the time being, and sometimes you smile at people on the street who never smile back. In an age where human interaction is essentially being reinvented, it's the small ways we empathize and create alongside one another that determine the future, not simply fantasizing a lovely version of it. Even as I write this, I'm reminded to *actually practice* such sentiments instead of merely ranting about it. In the end, that's what makes all the difference.

Mental Health

If the human psyche is the window through which we perceive life, then whether or not that window is damaged or cut off in some way influences the picture shown through it. Of course, maybe you think that analogy is cheesy, but you get the point. Mental health is probably one of the more sensitive topics for people to discuss due to how personal it is even on the broad spectrum that can explain it.

On one level, you have diagnosable mental illness, which is *such* a significant aspect of human life. Yet, to put it simply, we don't pay enough attention to it. When we do, it's usually *after* we see the damage caused by it, both individually, and on a societal level. It's no secret there's a lot of damaging perceptions about mental illness, but one of the most pressing is not even perceiving it at all, but rather sweeping broad issues of problems under the rug, often alienating those affected by them. It's sort of this attitude of, "if it doesn't affect me then I'm not gonna pay attention to it," which is actually the general attitude toward *a lot* of topics people are exposed to. Moreover, when people *are* somewhat willing to talk about mental illness, there tends to be conflicting ideas around what ailments to take seriously, and which to disregard as "exaggerated," to put it simply. Like, if a person is suicidal and expresses it, that's obviously extremely serious and needs to be addressed ASAP.

But if a person suffers from anxiety and expresses it, we sometimes lack *any* haste in giving them proper resources to deal with that. It's this thing where having less severe ailments like anxiety almost doesn't make you burdened enough in some eyes. Ironically, all this does is ensure they'll become *more* severe over time. Think of it this way; imagine having a heart attack versus breaking your arm. In both scenarios, yes, it's a wiser decision for a hospital staff to help the former before the latter. But if another doctor came in and said your arm is no big deal and would heal itself without giving you any treatment, you'd be pretty upset. In this case, being anxious is pretty normal and happens all the time right? So why bother freaking out over it?

I don't mean for this to sound like a PSA, but I think these are all colorless layers to the mind that are hard to neatly fit into words on a page. Mental illness has Influenced how humans perceive their world since the beginning really. To define and quantify what's "normal," and in turn "abnormal," has been hotly debated for as long as we've been able to conceptualize it. That being said, the notion of treating one's *mental* health with as much care as their *physical* health is a revelation slowly gaining traction in society these days. People better understand, both through personal development and observation, the importance of the mind and body as a single entity. Your brain is a muscle that works in heavy conjunction with the rest of your body. Injury to one segment is just as important as injury to the other. On a fundamental level, to *improve* the abilities of one, can in fact, benefit the health of the other. Diet, exercise, your physical environment, these are all elements of life that help us to better tap into the components of our minds. Likewise, your mental state affects how your body performs as well. Even something as small as your daily attitude can affect how your body feels as a vehicle. Just as there are an infinite number of things that can destroy us as humans, there are also boundless ways to train every aspect of our being simultaneously.

Ideally speaking, the same focus and tenacity that comes from either endeavor can translate to other human avenues, depending on how and when you apply them. It doesn't matter if you're sitting at a desk to work on a project, paying bills, completing a puzzle, or just giving attention to the people in your life, the option to refine every part of your existence is open to everyone. The asterisk comes into play when we confuse the limitations of some in a given area as weakness, or a failure on their part. Despite all the progress in mental health education, it's still pretty taboo in plenty of circles. I've seen firsthand plenty of communities where, to show you're burdened with mental illness is to show that you're a defect essentially. In some instances it's spoken, but often unspoken, that you not only serve no purpose to the wellbeing of the community, but also threaten to undermine it. For that reason, you're almost socially expelled until fixed to the liking of other's standards.

The fact of the matter is, life kind of runs like an RPG in many regards. What you may eventually realize is that stats may be *wildly* inconsistent for some players, but not to the fault of their own. The work and commitment they put into level up may come through far more abstract play styles than you're used to, but their willingness to grow could easily be seen as on par with anyone else's. To define what it means to win the game is relative to what you're aiming for. Honestly, I think a lot of people don't understand that when they're flexing their achievements or status nonstop.

Shifting gears a bit, I think it's worth recognizing mental health on other levels as well. Of course you have chemical imbalances akin to what I just talked about (albeit abstractly I admit), which can come from natural factors like genetics, or environmental ones (experiences, life events, even small little traumas). But I feel like mental fortitude is something *different* and often overlooked in how we traverse life and the worlds we live in. To put it bluntly, it's important to recognize mental health, break stigma, *and* support people that are just going through anything. *However*, across the board there *are* also just mentally weak people in the world, as harsh and contradictory to my earlier ideas as that sounds. There are mentally weak people in this world when it comes to everything they *do* have consistent control over; everything they actively have a choice in. Times often present themselves when we're fully aware of the optional paths laid out in front of us...and yet, some still choose ones of dysfunction, temptation, or even pettiness, despite knowing the consequences, often with some sort of twisted or half-baked justification that feigns accountability. That's not to be confused with *moments* of weakness now. We *all* have those days where you *know* what the right thing to do is, but you listen to the devil on your shoulder telling you the easy way out, whether that's out of fear, selfishness, laziness, or even times you doubt if you're good enough to handle something. No, I mean people who feed those demons consistently, even when they're given the opportunity to remedy it within themselves. People who fail to step up every time it matters the most. They're the ones who crumble under the pressure most notably.

Okay so all of that is obviously a very subjective and broad summary that can't possibly describe everyone that acts foolish in life. Humans are *far* more nuanced than that, as to distinguish what it means to be "weak," or "strong" is just as messy as "healthy," vs "unhealthy." If anything I'd concede it's more akin to weakness in the way of *morality* than any other form you could argue it manifests as. Regardless, I think that description serves as a common and overlooked denominator among many in this world. It's a universal constant across so many character archetypes, and to ignore that would be detrimental to everyone. To me, that constitutes *true* weakness.

To be fair, this could all be considered a questionable hot take, but I think it's because we naturally associate the idea of "weakness," with "worthlessness," when in reality, it's the exact opposite. Where there is weakness, there's also the potential to grow into something no one expects you to. To explore and nurture those fragile parts of your being across the board, mentally *and* physically, is to have faith in what you choose to become, regardless of your shortcomings. At the end of the day that's worth more than a lot of people realize. To be weak as I've described doesn't make you a lost cause to put it simply.

In hindsight, the reason some people don't understand this is due to another harsh truth about our health in society. Despite how optimal living your life like that and working on yourself may be, more than a lot of people in this world just don't have the resources to develop all the things that go into health and wellness. For instance, if you have a community of people severely limited economically, it shouldn't be surprising when they have fewer opportunities to develop an environment that fosters positive wellbeing, whether that be from lack of healthy grocery chains, effective schools in the area, poor infrastructure, or even community morale. Those factors have tremendous influence on people's worldview, making it much harder for *any* society to find balance between the mental and physical. How we improve these factors within our smallest societies usually has a ripple effect on larger realities through civilizations. Ultimately, the resulting influence is found in our human thought process, i.e., our ability to deduce meaningful information about life and our world as it evolves over time. From this flows greater ability to improve the quality of life at even the lowest level, as well as accurately recognize different mental states and the proper ways to address them.

Understand that our minds provide projections of reality, and what we see holds great influence over how we choose to conduct ourselves in everyday life. The balance we attempt to strike amongst ourselves is just one of the things that help give power to this. The body is undeniably an incredible vessel for the mind, yet imbalance in the relationship between the two yields a less than ideal existence, both on the individual and societal level. Funnily enough, trying to put such a sentiment into practice is easier said than done, but trust me when I say every ounce of effort you put into overcoming your aliments is worth the same as anyone else in this world, no matter what your stats are in life. In a world where such equilibrium is ever fleeting, choosing to take things day by day to align with where you want to be is a pursuit worth all the pain and trouble, even during times when you regress.

In my life I've met, known, and loved all different kinds of people who deal with mental illness, all the way from strangers to family. Yet it's been watching so many of them grow into amazing people despite what held them back that's taught me everything I speak on now. That proof of what's possible got me through *my own* dark times when I sincerely questioned if I could come back from it. Through those days, the hardest lesson for me to learn was that the health of your mind and body as a single entity exists on a multilayered spectrum. That means every aspect of who and what you are constantly play off each other day in and day out—engaging with the world around us, making connections we otherwise take for granted, inspiring one another. Some days it's still easier to see and feel this than others, but in the end, I also think that *knowing* those days will always come around is enough reason to have faith in that vision. It's enough to believe in that picture of reality.

What place does heroism actually have among humankind?

I think it's safe to say human beings have told stories about heroes, villains, and everything in between since our early history. It's ingrained in everything from our literature to music to artwork when you think about it. We've always been naturally drawn to the idea of a savior who stands for something noble and respectable. Likewise, we've always been intrigued by the entity of a villain who threatens to undermine those values. What's interesting is how, at least in my eyes, that fascination has been revitalized in the last 20 years or so.

Now, to be clear it shouldn't come as a surprise that I'm a nerd, and a reserved one at that. A good portion of the entertainment I enjoy has always come from stories with superhero lore or something akin to that embodying them. As a kid I was all about Spider-Man and random comics that seemed cool to me. I didn't even pay *too* much attention to the themes of some of the plots. As I got older though I became more enamored with manga, anime, and of course superhero movies as a whole given how well known their rise in popularity is. Don't get me wrong though, I was into plenty of other things while growing up, but the eccentric interpretations of what heroism entailed through different mediums always interested me.

Honestly, I think it's important to ask what defines a hero in life, mainly because of the varied hero archetypes represented through our societies and the many stories that have kept them alive. At the heart of it all is the question of what defines different layers of justice or injustice. What is just? What is unjust in our existence as sentient lifeforms? Honestly, I'd say the answer is entirely subjective. What we deem as right and wrong evolves over time after all. Heroes tend to serve as an affirmation to those morals and ethics. I will say though, the conceptual integration of hero and villain stories through different time periods kind of goes back to the issue of black and white thinking in society. The former representing the ideal and the latter representing what's reprehensible. Yet, despite those who hold absolute beliefs, I think in today's age most people realize that heroes and villains don't automatically embody pure good and evil respectively. That's *partially* why heroism has become more interesting lately, because the lines are far less clear at the end of the day.

These days our stories and entertainment offer more grounded interpretations on heroes, even when certain plots or worlds are inherently mystical. Although, as someone who's often analytical of them, I *really* appreciate when writers establish that balance in a way that lets you empathize and relate with their characters, yet also provides the reader with a sense of escapism, but I digress. As a whole, they deeply explore the psychological spectrum of humans (or just sentient beings in general) wielding extraordinary abilities, as well as the psychology of societies affected by them. What's funny is despite the many entertaining and thought-provoking stories we indulge in, I actually don't believe much of the vigilantism paired with them would ever be a good thing for our societies at all. Like, I grew up on Spider-Man, The Avengers, and later Batman, The Justice League, etc., but I still always thought of how implausible being a vigilante would be in real life, superpowered or not.

Hear me out for a second. If you were to go up every level of law or government, you can legitimately keep asking, "what makes this person, or these people qualified to distinguish right from wrong?" That goes for any community, society, state, or country. In reality you could spend all day going down the rabbit hole of how subjective human ethics are, especially considering how contradictory they can be between different groups of ourselves. Thing is, by nature the power to judge, sentence and execute usually corrupts and destroys when solely left in the hands of even the *most* well intentioned. That's partially why in the real world, vigilantes would exist on a *far* more slippery slope toward corruption than our normal institutes of justice like regular police or military, who we already debate about regarding how they should be used and to what extent. If you had both vigilantes and normal law enforcement present in a similar way depicted in fiction, even non superpowered ones would represent a *huge* imbalance in power. Assuming secret identities are in the mix, you're essentially playing a waiting game to see how long before those split personas conflict with each other. There's a reason identity crises are so repetitively used as storylines after all. You could honestly take heroes like Batman or Spiderman as perfect examples of this through the *decades* they've been fleshed out. Being a one-person force against whatever you oppose inevitably pulls you in a different direction from normal life that comes with *far* less burdens in comparison. As a whole, the dichotomies between hero and civilian usually result in two personas in conflict with each other, each trying to go in opposite directions. Sooner or later you have to give in to one or be torn apart by both. Someone like Bruce Wayne inadvertently becomes the artificial mask to the Dark Knight that is Batman. Likewise, the responsibilities of being Spider-man and protecting those who, in many instances, don't even appreciate him, ultimately leads to turmoil in the life of Peter Parker. In real life anyone dealing with similar burdens as those two would run the risk of becoming pretty unhinged (which is also explored for both characters very nicely in certain storylines if you're about that comic life). In short, trying to exist as multiple entities in that way comes at a cost, as it can tear you apart little by little from the psychological trauma accumulating over time. It's because of this that concentrating preventive power into the hands of one entity *so* unbalanced with others (i.e. police, military, etc.), it inevitably produces real world instability not so easily retconned like in fiction. You essentially become a wild card in the delegation of order and chaos, crime and peace, Danger and safety, etc., creating greater problems than would persist in your absence. Honestly that even goes for heroes who *don't* rely on secret identities, like Captain America, or groups that operate privately like The Avengers, Fantastic Four, Justice League, etc. The reason we don't usually apply this thinking to fictional heroes to this is simple. Between writing, marketing, and reputation, the audience, at least on a subconscious level, will usually acknowledge the hero as being most capable of solving certain problems, even if they were brought about by them in hindsight. Deep down we *know* there's some sort of pay off, some sort of greater narrative that *needs* to be heard...but that's not always the case in reality.

Now, I wouldn't blame you for criticizing my use of comic lore as a lens for all this. It's really to show how so many different story beats don't translate to the real world. The truth is, human beings really would fear Superman more than revere him if he were real. Even *if* his intentions were noble in hindsight, what is there to challenge a god's notion of right, wrong and everything in between? The same goes for other omega level beings who, again, we as the audience are persuaded to trust as the greatest source of resolution to certain problems, even when we acknowledge those beings don't always have the best judgment to begin with.

Perhaps it's paradoxical then that those same sentiments of heroism are so essential to humankind in the long run.

See, by nature we're *all* susceptible to evil and corruption, yet also magnificent benevolence, regardless if you have power in society or not. The temptation to satisfy primal and selfish desires in the face of ethical standards has always been a part of who we are as a species. It speaks to a special kind of self-preservation throughout history, having taken on different forms of course. I mean, obviously it's not always cute and cuddly to talk about, but honestly, some of the more abhorrent behaviors we've had and still exhibit is fascinating to study depending on what perspective you employ. What's more, we're often more inclined to play devil's advocate against principles of what we deem ideal or heroic than we realize. I actually think this correlates to how we generally tend to perceive antagonists, or villains within both fictional and nonfictional media. We're drawn to the ones a small part of us can relate to, even if we're rooting against them, or if they're rounded characters themselves. Simply put, we enjoy following the villains that most closely resemble our dark side. For me, I always love a villain who has a sick or twisted philosophy that you can't initially refute because they're kind of right when you analyze their thinking. The kind that aren't necessarily a one to one antithesis of the protagonist personality wise, but rather a dark counterpart to what they stand for in the story.

On the flip side, it's hard to argue humans haven't come a long way despite this. You can't deny that in some way we've found universal truth in what's humane among our species through everything that's subjective. What's overlooked is how that progression is rarely linear, often moving forward in a zigzag motion. The same principle applies to our individual development as well. It's not a straight line toward refinement in the long run. Going forward requires us to reflect on the past, be self-aware of the present, and choose how to shape the future in response to both. Who and what do we choose to be as a result of what's already said and done? Out of the very best and worst of humanity we become that which we feed, giving power to different mindsets, behaviors, and attitudes that persist through generations. That's part of the reason for so many varied walks of life that exist and connect in this world. It's a reality that's always found a way to persist despite how small minded we can be at times.

In general, the nature of heroism serves as encouragement to course correct from those small minded, often destructive tendencies. That's the case both in a literal sense where you'd save someone from physical harm, or in a philosophical sense because of what you stand for as an entity, how you build up others, etc. In essence, what we *can* take from comics, superhero movies and other fiction lie in between the lines of such stories. The existence of beings who at least *try* to course correct an environment that zigs when it's supposed to zag. Now, despite its validity, the slight caveat with that idea is how you could argue it justifies opposing ideals when isolated from each other. If someone from another country proposes change that benefits *their* society, yet conflicts with the ideals of your own, is it really fair to label them as malicious or villainous right off the bat? Like I said before, the power to decide how reality should be course corrected in even the *smallest* ways is a power that gets messier the more layers you uncover. It's especially true considering that most of what I'm saying is just scratching the surface for how we truly embrace heroism. For instance, these days you'll see a lot more comics and shows explore the politics of a hero filled society. In some plotlines heroes are celebrities with their likeness monetized. In others, we see the more nuanced side of law enforcement and how that plays out among what are essentially super soldiers governing common man, similar to how I described earlier. What's interesting is, just like with a person's integrity, the essence of being called a "hero" essentially becomes diluted, and eventually corrupted in many of these tales.

I think a real hero is someone with that self-awareness how they could easily slide across the spectrum of good or evil. In fiction you see characters like Batman and Superman for instance, who are presented as completely different in their approaches toward justice yet are both introspective about this. Characters like that are sometimes written to be *self-aware* of how unbalanced their existence is with the rest of reality. They're written to intentionally *limit* themselves as a result of that. As a result of being susceptible to corruption. Comics and hero fiction, *despite* plenty of eccentric themes, teach us to mitigate this as best we can in our lifetimes, even when the endeavor seems fruitless, or when the sacrifices we make go unrecognized. The phrase, "with great power comes great responsibility," is cliche and overused for a reason. Real heroes step up to that responsibility of such standards *beyond* basic discipline, even when they get nothing out of it in the long run. Even when they *know* there's no reward or recognition at the end of the tunnel. They're the ones who wake up every day and decide to be a better human being than the last in order to see that through. They choose to build up the best part of who they are while acknowledging and controlling the worst parts, even when feeling underappreciated, or doubting the motivations behind their own pursuits. Even when those negative mindsets arise, they'll at least try to pass such dedication along to others. It's choosing to either build up or tear down those around you, in *addition* to yourself, that signifies someone who goes above and beyond in their lifetime. I think that idea is universal among *all* the angles of justices we can perceive in this world.

Truthfully, most of us aren't heroes. Very few in this world find the balance in existing as one. The ones that do are usually the ones you never hear about. The good news is that through everything standing the test of time among humans in this universe, sooner or later just about everyone has a chance to be heroic. Against all the dread within ourselves, and among *all* the unfair power dynamics and hierarchies, we all have the potential to be more. To spend a lifetime paying attention to what we build up or tear down among each other in this universe and be conscious of such influence is what gives us the chance to realize it. It's something I believe everyone has felt at least once in their life, even if just for a moment. Vigilantes may be ineffective in real life, but it's what we see them try to stand for that draws us into their thinking. They represent the *spark* of an *idea*, and in societies where even the most ordinary people see corruption, that *means* something, even at the risk of it leading to fire. Despite heroism rarely being embraced in the grand scheme of things, it prevails enough that we still appreciate and contemplate it at this present moment in human history. Among that history, it will forever be a universal constant. That much, I have faith in.

Discovering the world outside of you reveals your level of influence on it- An encouragement to travel abroad

Okay, so a large part of this chapter is going to consist of me finally addressing the very title of this book (I know, took me long enough didn't it?). But yeah, I'm pretty introverted to be quite honest. To a large extent I was shy as a kid, and plenty of people could probably see that, but there's a difference between being shy and being introverted. The latter is my personality type in general and being shy was just part of the package growing up. As a whole it can be a double-edged sword depending on how you look at it. Although recently I stumbled across an interesting general explanation for introversion while online one day. It's not my idea, but it basically poses the notion that for some people, the challenge of being introverted isn't that you *dislike* interacting with people, but rather you dislike having *meaningless* interactions with people. In fairness, that might be common sense for some, but for myself it's the closest description of what I've felt most of my life if I'm being honest. It had just been put into more concise words than I had ever thought to use.

What you could describe as meaningless in this context may vary from person to person, but for me, it's things like having small talk with someone new that you can *clearly* tell is going nowhere fast. It's also when you know someone won't even remember your name the next time you see them, or how about just icebreaker/get to know you activities in general during events right? The most *interesting fact* I can think about myself on the spot is that I make a nice pasta dish...yeah I can literally feel my will to live slowly decay during those. There's also when you know a conversation is only happening with someone because of some obligation neither of you really want to fulfill in the first place...the list goes on! Usually my intuition tells me when these kinds of things are more likely to occur, and so I'm more inclined to keep to myself, and I'd say that's been my subconscious thought process throughout my life honestly. But like I said, it's a double-edged sword when I also acknowledge the part of myself that's always been overly curious about different people and ways of life. Despite being introverted, I still developed a special reverence for exploration as I got older and got to visit new places. The more time that passed, the more of the world I got to see, yet I also realized how much I'd never understood or experienced.

I'm opening up about all of this because it's worth discussing how much crossover exists in the way of ideas, as well as the intersection of lives in this world. Most people would probably agree with this on a surface level, but it's not until you make an effort to physically travel throughout this globe that you experience this crossover firsthand, or at least that's what I've deduced through my own travels. I mean, think about it. The entire concept of human transportation was only refined to be expedient in the past two hundred years or so. That's a mere moment in the grand timeline of human existence. We've made exponential progress in how we live together on an international level, but there's still a plethora of knowledge for us to share with each other. We take it for granted in all honesty. On a daily basis we move across the globe repeatedly, and when it's not physically, it's digitally. You could argue that human beings are more connected now than ever, and I'd agree with that assessment, but in many ways I don't think we *truly* recognize how valid that is. It really doesn't matter where you are, but literally everything you do as a sentient being affects the existing world around you, including all the other lifeforms in it from other people to plants. It sounds pretty meta to say *everything* in life is connected, but I'd say such a statement is self-evident when you take the time to traverse the many networks of interaction we embrace on a daily basis.

Truthfully, one of the ways I've realized this in life has been through food...I love food, and I absolutely *love* to eat. Between that, cooking, and traveling, I grew up learning to appreciate how something so fundamental, and perhaps minute to some people, has connected civilizations throughout time. When you're talking about travel, either today or centuries ago, it's not infrequent to learn about someone bringing an exotic kind of sustenance into a new area. Christopher Columbus is the vanilla example for this we all learn about in grade school for instance. You're ultimately left with these societal crossovers creating chain reactions that benefit humankind, albeit with new problems that have ripple effects within their own right of course, like genocide at the hands of that last example, but I digress. Travel leads to sharing food among people. Sharing food leads to the introduction of different diets. Different diets introduce different qualities of living and health amongst people. New health conditions lead to new scientific developments and interpretation on how to live our lives. Surely you could list many more influences that I'm missing here, but you get the point. All it takes is for one person to create a new dish from experimenting before it's introduced to new people, and everything else follows suit throughout a whole society.

It's easy to see this as one *small* example of how subtle actions can produce long term change throughout the world. It's the presence of such ripple effects throughout time that shape our reality, influencing how we perceive the subtle nuances of our lives and societies, like attitudes about food for instance. Small or large scale, their impact persists both through our individual actions and as a singular species, living among many. In hindsight, I didn't fully appreciate any of this when I was a kid. It wasn't until I started to travel more when I got older I began to understand the dual nature of the fire embodying this species more clearly. Our drive to exist for more than just procreation, like fire, is just as capable of destruction as it is creation. It was having to accept both the best *and* worst of what every environment had to offer that got me through the anxiety of traveling and all the risks that come with it. It just isn't plausible to look at one without the other.

What makes that all worthwhile is doing it alongside people who help you appreciate the vastness of this world, both in the physical and metaphorical sense. Don't get me wrong, sometimes you need to go under the radar and journey alone, but as someone with a natural instinct to withdraw inward, most of the people I *actually needed* in my life and on my travels

PHILOSOPHY OF AN INTROVERT

came without me asking. Plus, traveling with other people is just more fun than going alone if I'm being frank. At the end of the day, those people help you grow into a greater force of nature than you would be without them. The more you grow, the easier it becomes to see universal phenomenon play out no matter where you are in the world. Regardless of race, culture, gender, you're better able to recognize not only common human behavior, but how that behavior is put out into the universe, along with its impact and overlap. But the key is seeing it within yourself first. When you understand that even your smallest actions and attitudes have a domino effect on the rest of the world, and when you embrace that with the intention of developing who you are, you begin to foster more meaningful interactions with those who cross your path, even if it's only for a short time. You will, I believe, feel how broadly reality is connected to you on a daily basis. I think that's one of the biggest takeaways from traveling if I'm being frank. In many ways it forces you to be uncomfortable and choose how you want to exist in this world, something we often push to the back of our minds when we get too accustomed to the realities of one given place.

    Thinking about all of this as I sit here and write also has me questioning how our practical influence on the larger universe will change over time as we explore more of it. I mean, outside of science fiction, humanity has traveled through *very* little of the cosmos firsthand. I know it's a question that's been done to death the past few years, but what *would* we look like as a multi planet species? What does humanity look like If it were possible to truly *exist* in other places like that long term. Personally, I think at the *very* least, human beings will eventually become capable of scavenging other planets for economic/resource purposes. That's assuming earth is definitively the only suitable rock for us to consistently live and evolve on long term. Although, that's just an assumption, and you know what they say about assuming.

Regardless, having the ability to traverse the universe more thoroughly is something I believe will come to pass along with human advancement. If you consider the mere act of exploration by humans from the very beginning of our history, you'll notice it produced different groups of people living in different regions of the globe. Long story short, you have different members of an intelligent species evolving in different ways, partially based on location, along with the unique ways they interacted with those environments. By the time people started going overseas, what they found seemed like different worlds all on their own. The resulting crossover in turn helped begin some of the ugliest, but also most beautiful ages in human history across thousands of years. I think when we reflect on this phenomenon, it's easy to see the possibility of such behavior patterns playing out on an intergalactic scale (and no, I don't mean some Star Wars like reality). What I mean is, even if we never end up *directly* living on other planets, the human experience will still take place on them to an extent where consciousness branches out more broadly, and evolves in different ways for the better. When such an occurrence comes to pass, I believe the answer to what ripple effect we have on the universe will be just a touch clearer. Moreover, everything we choose to do today in this generation is connected to how we envision that future. It's because of its uncertainty that the future exists in both a state of prosperity and tragedy simultaneously.

That being said, in the short term I think it's irrelevant where you are on the scale of introversion to extroversion. The way you insert yourself into foreign environments is what helps strengthen such connections that weave your future, even at the smallest level. Of course, it helps not to be *too* complacent on either end. Closing yourself off from the rest of the world also closes off your mind from learning of its many intricacies. Inversely I've admittedly met more extroverted people mainly enamored with the "touristy" side of traveling, which isn't bad on its own, but there's so many more layers to bear witness to when it comes to other ways of life, societal frameworks, ideas, etc.

At the heart of it all though, all life exists in an interconnected web of causality, whether we're paying attention to it or not. To feel connected, and see such universal phenomena play out has been intriguing for someone like me. It's also been pretty fun when I look back on some of my misadventures, both alone and with others. For as much trouble as you can get into in this world, you kind of have to have a laughable misadventure every now and again. Being able to laugh and smile, both at yourself and what's going on around you helps us appreciate some of the more wholesome things in this world. I remember the times in my life where I was especially pessimistic and cynical about humanity, easily seeing the worst in not just the world around me, but myself as well. Ultimately though, it's been the different walks of life that have shown me there is true beauty in the eye of all the chaos that envelopes life itself. What it means to experience that beauty for oneself is different for everyone, but the potential to do so is just one of the *many* things that help connect all of us as not only human beings, but as one of many species continuously experiencing what the universe has to offer. Helping each other get even a *brief* glimpse of that in this lifetime is probably the most meaningful thing one could ask for by the end of it.

Now on to a less than stellar topic to keep you awake. Politics: an essential yet also silly part of civil society

Alright, let's address the elephant in the room. Politics can be a divisive and messy topic in today's world. However, the fact that we govern ourselves as an intelligent species literally makes it an essential component of life, and the same could probably be said for other species in the animal kingdom as well to be honest. Coincidentally, this chapter is being written during an election year here in the U.S., 2020 to be exact. Generally speaking, the shift in politics leading to this election has yielded just about every political hot take, theory, or commentary you could anticipate and then some. What's interesting among all the talk are mainly our attitudes surrounding what makes America an ideal society among many, and how we act on them as people.

For starters, I'll admit that when I was a kid, I honestly never understood the concept of the American dream. I mean, it was easy to view as the prime ideal to embrace in this country of course, that much I was able to grasp. On paper, all the patriotic and noble components of western society sound great, and to a large degree they are. I mean, the mores of phrases like 'freedom' and 'justice' have evolved to be synonymous with America in some capacity after all. Yet even with kid me knowing the importance of that stuff, I couldn't put my finger on why my sense of patriotism always felt, well, different from most people. Looking back, I can tell it was mainly because I saw a difference in the pride that embodies American values in comparison with the underlying execution of them in certain pockets of society. In a way this sort of curbed my enthusiasm about being an American as a young child if I'm being honest. What turned me off was the easily observable contradictions in society that made such ideals feel more and more like *just* a dream. None of this is to say I don't *currently* appreciate what's possible in this country, but rather that I've spent a large part of my life learning about the discrepancy between what America is, versus what America is supposed to be.

There's pretty much no denying that all the human rights used to organize the country in its early beginnings are noble in nature. If you've ever taken time to see how some of those rights are oppressed in other developed *and* underdeveloped countries, it's easy to see why a place like America benefits from embracing things like freedom of speech, due process, individuality, etc. Despite that, something I've consistently noticed in the attitudes of Americans, and especially politicians, is the notion that being the pioneers of such ideas puts us a step above everyone else in the world. The upper echelon of being human if you will. Of course, that's not indicative of everyone, and is subjective, but I think it's fair to say plenty fit that description. It's also fair to point out how easy it is to buy into that idea if you're an American yourself. What's intriguing, however, is how this looks from an outside perspective. Take the gun debate for example (I know, very smart for me to choose one of the most controversial topics). Obviously, the use and abuse of firearms isn't exclusive to western countries, but it's our attitudes toward having and protecting this power that America holds a reputation for to some degree. Simply put, we straight up argue over the essence of guns and their implication in a manner I feel is far more existential than other societies in comparison. In essence, the topic has morphed into a dialogue consisting of *far* more layers than originally intended when America was founded. Healthcare systems are another good example when you consider how our knowledge of basic human anatomy, technology, medicine, and even the *ethics* of medicine have changed. To contemplate the value of not just human life, but all life, has become a deeper rabbit hole over the past few centuries. This is the case with a whole range of issues when you think about it. In reality, it's only natural to happen over time in a developing nation. Whatever ways people choose to mold society, much of its advancements will be supported by that society's values as the fundamental building blocks.

Truth be told you could probably argue this is only second to economic ventures in a place like the U.S., but either way it's a comparable pillar among any nation. Business primarily drives innovation amongst groups of people, no matter how big or small. When you consider ideas that propel humankind, societies are generally harder pressed to incorporate them among the masses if it doesn't significantly contribute to a marketplace, regardless of how much it benefits humanity. Point blank: even the best medicines will be ignored if they're not making someone some money somewhere. Furthermore, those innovations won't be improved upon unless a level of economic competition is present as an incentive for the innovators and businesses alike. This concept really isn't anything new or complicated though. Elements of it are present in a lot of countries, but I think we often forget what a key characteristic it is in western society by itself, *and* on the international scale.

When we combine this economic drive with prioritizing societal values, what you're left with is the branding of America as the land of opportunity. All things considered, this country has grown a lot under such a mindset, yet I still take issue with people who vehemently claim that America is the greatest country in the world. A lot of arguments I've heard in favor of this cite how it's because of everything America has grown into that we live in the most progressive periods in human history. That includes all the commentary on freedom, constitutional frameworks, and noble sacrifice one could touch on in defense of that idea. Personally, I agree with all of that. I mean hey, despite my confusion as a kid, I'd be the only one that would stand for the pledge of allegiance in school. I... feel like a socially awkward dork just reminiscing about it in fact. Nevertheless, I think it's worth remembering that several different microcosms exist within the United States in terms of quality of life. Communities where life doesn't always align with the ideals of what America should be, even in the presence of whatever laws and policies our government believes are best for the people. Obviously racial inequality is the first thing that comes to mind regarding this given how deeply ingrained it is in our history. To be honest it's probably one of our more prevalent traits concerning the hubris of humans, which is ironic considering how multicultural America is. For many of us in this world, our genetics are literally blends of different heritages put together over generations, both voluntarily, and *involuntary*. In addition to race, you also have communities developed with opposing cultures as well. Not always in a confrontational way, but in social principles and norms, even when they're in the same state or city. You know, places where you'd go settle down to have a family and lead a simple life versus a more busy place where the nightlife is loud and lively, i.e. easy small town living vs large city living as just one basic example. Both communities have different needs for a variety of different people based on race, class, sexuality, etc., having only grown in scale over the past 250 years or so. In many ways, everyone has ideas for what's best for them respectively, yet often butt heads on how to implement policies and change that don't only benefit one at the expense of another.

In retrospect, 2020 has been an interesting case study showing how all these realms are connected. Most notably, a global health pandemic caused by COVID-19, a coronavirus, upended the lives of thousands of people in just a few months, creating a domino effect that changed the lifestyle of many different groups of people moving forward. Exponential infection rates led to mass quarantine. Quarantine led to drastic shifts in business both domestically and internationally. And consequently, these shifts simultaneously disrupted the social, economic, and even mental patterns of every demographic you could think of, whether it be on the basis of race, sexual identity, age, class, etc. As you could imagine, government response on the state and federal level in the U.S was under high scrutiny, and the politics of how to move forward are *still* hotly debated even at the time of writing this. In a philosophical sense, you could say the makeup of our society showed how vulnerable it truly was. Not merely in the way of physical health, but in the way of uncivil discourse that was amplified as time went on. Growing racial tensions, police brutality, and other high-profile disasters that occurred thereafter also helped define the existential dread of many Americans that year in particular, myself included. Bluntly speaking, despite not being the outright *worst* crisis in history, things fell apart pretty fast, and that was the demoralizing part. The fact that despite all our notions of grandeur, it only took a few short months for things to hit the fan. It didn't take much to upend many of our foundations. Not irreversibly, but in a way where most would be affected by the fallout somehow.

That's not to paint a picture of *total* dystopia, however. In reality it's only *natural* to have pockets of dysfunction scattered within communities, states, and countries. There's no such thing as a utopia after all. At the same time, I don't think it's unfounded to say the thin veneer of our society could use some refinement. What interests me are all the people who claim to have the cure to all its problems. Politicians probably come to the forefront of this, considering they're the ones basically *tasked* with keeping civilization afloat. As a whole, to help run a human society is a task directly connecting not just your actions and policies, but who you are as a person to all of humanity in some way, shape, or form. Thing is, by nature politics are *all* the ways we engage with systems affecting our self-governance. That's only made *more* complicated in an expanding age of information to be exact. As we develop our worlds and the connections binding them, it's always a game adding more players and levels to consider when making moves. To say I'd want to study the hallmarks of this era if I were from the future is an understatement, mainly because the psychology of these people is fascinating despite how utterly *silly* politics can be. Personally I think there's a large, underlying presence of narcissism that guides many of them on the global scale. Funnily enough, I don't feel this is such a detrimental characteristic. Everyone's got some ego to be honest. The problem is, when we're talking about those among ourselves seeking to be qualified to govern, much of their own ego is projected onto a body of human consciousness they're fully aware they hold influence over (i.e., the people). The presence of this power alone is just as capable of corrupting a nation as it is to propel one. Needless to say, human beings have held a tumultuous relationship with power since the beginning of our existence. At its core, such an essence can be defined as the ability to influence something in any manner that bends to your will, even if it's just a little. This can range from pushing someone in a fight when you were five, to using rhetoric to elicit a reaction out of just one person in a crowd as a politician. It's an ability all of us have, and one we've played with from the start. Even subconsciously, people understand they're capable of influencing attitudes, ideas, the atmosphere of a room, etc. Yet I'd argue these intangible expressions of power can corrupt to varying degrees by amplifying the worst parts of who you are if you're not careful, which many politicians aren't. That doesn't mean all of them are trash leaders completely unfit for their jobs (although you could find many through history who fit that description). Rather, our leaders who at times perceive themselves as gods are just as susceptible to human nature as your local coffee barista. The same goes for a nation that acts as a single entity in relation to others in an International forum. For a country like America, our collective attitudes comprise both civilians and those with political power alike, contributing to our reputation.

Honestly, when contemplating the U. S's position in the international arena, I think it helps to view it from the perspective of a school system. By that I mean, imagine you have a classroom full of kids, with one of them often regarded as the smartest. For one thing, intelligence isn't expressed the exact same way in every person. Some people are more proficient in certain areas of life than others, but it doesn't automatically make them *inferior*. You'll see that play out in a class among kids being compared to one another. But, for argument's sake, let's imagine a scenario where a child is definitively smarter than everyone else in their class. Regardless of the difference between them and their peers, I don't think it's a stretch to say it means nothing if the child isn't working to live up to their full potential. Now, on one hand, not every smart kid is going to walk around with this in mind on a day to day basis. Kids get lazy sometimes and aren't always motivated to fulfill something sounding oh so virtuous, trust me, it's normal. But on the other hand, if the same kid constantly spends their time coasting through school as they age, it's problematic. Even if they can get better test scores than everyone else without trying, or secure all the best achievements that look good on paper, are they really successful if they're not working toward their full capabilities? I think of the U.S. in this context and in relation to so many other places and societies in the world.

Our nation is still young in the grand scheme of things, with so much potential. Yet we have a history of inconsistency when fulfilling it. At the end of the day, America is a great country, but it's nowhere as great as it could be. That might be obvious for some, but it's the dismissal of the steps needed to make it better that ultimately holds it back. By steps, I truly don't mean complying with the ideology of *every* person on twitter who thinks they know how to fix the world, nor does it mean choosing a side that makes you appear intellectual. I mean focusing on the nuance that can be found in the many worldviews seeking to be heard and trying to find the universal constants among them. Truth is an essence spread amongst the consciousness of many people in this world. All just different pieces of the same puzzle that is life. I think when we try to unite those truths, or at least condense them, we're better able to move forward in answering the question of how to fulfill our potential. Not just in one country like America, but globally as well. I know that sounds in line with the cliche of "let's all just work together," but hey, cliches stand the test of time for a reason. Things get interesting when those lessons reinvent themselves based on the era you're living in, political or otherwise.

The intricacies of word choice can sometimes be an enigma

If I'm being straightforward, the concept of language was actually *another* topic that seemed strange to me as a kid. It's funny because in learning things like grammar, sentence structure, etc., I never understood *where* exactly words came from. I'm not joking when I say that I legitimately thought at some point in time, every word in the English language was voted into becoming an official word by a council of people who had a big fancy meeting about it. What was even better was how I eventually realized how paradoxical that was, ultimately just confusing myself to no end as I would ponder over this for days. If that were the case, how would this council have started communicating with each other before the first phrase was ever invented? Yeah I know that sounds really stupid (for *many* reasons), but again...I was an interesting child. Nevertheless, I don't think it's a stretch to say that language in general, not *just* English, is quite fascinating when you consider how multifaceted sentient communication has been throughout our history.

One of the things I've found most interesting in the general scope of language is word choice, both verbally and written. It sounds basic, but the words we use serve as powerful tools in how we interact with each other and the world itself.

Words and phrases illicit ideas. Ideas inspire actions. Actions influence the reality we all live in. You'll see this is true throughout all languages when you think about it, although I must admit, I'm not multilingual myself despite talking about it. I mean, I can speak a fair amount of Spanish, and know a few bits and pieces of Italian and Thai, but that's about it. Regardless, learning the history of how different languages have evolved intrigues me, especially when you realize how influential migration has been through much of it. Basic English as it stands today is pretty much an amalgam of other language elements. Add that to the countless accents and dialects around the world, and you're left with a rich history of what are essentially weird sounds we make with our mouths to further our existence. Honestly, it's kind of cool when you think about it from an evolutionary standpoint.

All that being said, we still miscommunicate with each other on a daily basis. Given how complex our thoughts, intentions, and motivations may be, we sometimes neglect the ever-changing context of both our words, and the situations they're paired with, often perceiving a given message with rigid interpretations of its meaning. Text messaging and messaging through apps in general is a perfect example of this I mentioned earlier. At one point or another we've all gone a bit far in trying to read between the lines of a given message. Everyone has their ideas of how to phrase a lengthy paragraph during an argument, or how long they should wait to reply to even the nicest message. At the end of the day, you could have a whole conversation with someone and so many sentiments are lost in translation by the end of it. The same goes for social media as a whole, albeit the public nature of it opens many more doors to miscommunication *and* misrepresentation. What's interesting is how different storylines and narratives are influenced or created by different communication styles and how they captivate us, whether it be for the better or worse. You could also take legal jargon as another example of this. So much of it deals with the specific wording of concepts to support a given argument that tells a story. A lot of times it's used in a way to find loopholes and keep people from being *technically* liable in certain events, i.e., operating on technicalities via definitions. That's what happens when you have powerful members of a society keen on how collective groups define certain scenarios.

The problem is, you'll find that there are exceptions for the context we put *so many* of our words *and* ideas in. Ignoring this is what eventually leads to those all or nothing mindsets. Little by little they add up to make those black and white hot takes. If the term "murder" is *always* followed by someone who deserves punishment, then how do we approach a situation of pure self-defense for one's life? Likewise if the phrase "illegal" is *always* an indication that someone is a criminal, and if being a "criminal" is always associated with being a bad person, how do you deal with someone who thought they had no other choice, and may be a decent person at heart? It's not that we use these words that's a problem, but rather the *limited sentiments* attached to them. Such thinking ultimately shuts out room for critical thought we could share with each other when we interact. See, if you can't adapt your language and speech to evolving realities, then your ability to refine your thinking suffers as a result.

Granted, I think there are plenty of people who understand this yet use such understanding to manipulate others. You could argue people like politicians would be pretty good at that given how rhetoric is almost a prerequisite in politics. The art of persuasion as they call it is used on many levels, and the ability to spin or isolate certain parts of a given concept to reinforce your own idea is powerful indeed. Of course, other institutions and regular people in general, not just figures like politicians, know how to do this on a *subtle* level, ultimately directing an interaction or engagement in their favor. It all depends on knowledge regarding the listener or audience. You could probably even point to some of the word choice used in this chapter as a real-world example. Surely someone reading this could think of different words or phrases to articulate everything I'm saying right now.

I don't mean to make this an English lesson, especially given how intricate other languages are as I've already alluded to, but hopefully you have an idea on how malleable the essence of communication is as it exists between humans, at least as it pertains to word choice. This is barely including other forms of communication such as body language, facial expressions, or even just reading the room sometimes. Things like gestures, a pause, micro expressions, *hand* expressions—they can all be manipulated, customized, and presented in a manner that influences any given outcome even to the smallest degree.

Personally, I've always found those nuances pretty intriguing to spot through something as simple as people watching for instance. Not in a creepy way of course, but more in an analytical manner. In the context of communication, it's usually interesting to observe people in an enclosed space, a group setting like a restaurant or workspace for instance. In those scenarios where you're in close proximity with other people, you can differentiate what they say from how they subtly act if you're paying attention. For example, say you're at a restaurant with three other people, the four of you sitting in a square formation. If you notice that the two people across from you have their bodies shifted in the direction of the one next to you while they converse, and divert their eyes and head away from you as *you* converse, it may be an indication they find your neighbors input to be more captivating in that moment, despite there being a back and forth dialogue. Of course, that's a pretty general inference I'm using as an example. I mean, who knows, maybe you're annoying, maybe you look weird in a certain outfit, I don't know. They could straight up just not want to be around you for whatever stupid reason, but the point is, when you're in such personal settings, being able to analyze those small physical expressions provides insight on people's attitudes to certain things. Something so simple as raising an eyebrow, looking exasperated, amused, or just indifferent, can all show that our messages hold deeper meaning than their surface portrayal. Sometimes they don't translate into genuine sentiments, and other times they're more affirmative than what we say outright. In short, we use words to validate our body language and vice versa. In many ways it's akin to a feedback loop when you think about it.

 In the same way we're capable of manipulating words for personal gain, they also work against us in revealing underlying social realities. A coworker who says, "good morning," to everyone in the office, but only "mornin," while barely audible to the guy one cubicle over yonder may seem like nothing but pettiness, until you overhear that they dated for two years at one point and the breakup didn't go so well, then it all starts to makes sense.

On a deeper level of this, there's also the matter of slang. While that may seem a bit of a random topic to bring up, I find it compelling to view how closely related human slang follows the principle of reinvention. In this way, social realities play a role in such development. No matter where you go, the slang people will use in a given region is always changing as time goes on, whether it's due to trends, social movements, or even just a different sense of humor embraced by certain people. At its core, slang is generally based on universally shared sentiments within a given group. We simply pair these sentiments with specific sounds as a quicker way of expressing them. I say "sounds" because a lot of times the slang people use aren't even full or actual words (I'm guilty of doing this when speaking too). Regardless, it makes up a large percentage of how different populations speak to one another. In plenty circles you'd get some weird looks if you're out with friends and only spoke properly as your language dictates. In the same way normal conversing elicits certain responses, so can slang depending on who you're talking to. In a way, some people can better empathize with a given attitude you might emit when using slang naturally. I think that's just basic psychology on some level to be honest. We're more likely to develop affinity with someone at least *capable* of communicating on the same level as us.

That being said, such capability may change and evolve as trends come and go over time. In my own experience, I can think of distinct periods throughout my time in school where certain slang was the main way kids would talk to each other, and it would subtly change throughout elementary, middle, high school, and college. I don't think it's a stretch to say if you hear someone talk using outdated slang, they *might* be a different age group than you. It's kind of the stereotypical "old school," versus "new school," way of connecting. But again, such reinvention of trends is natural for human beings to reinforce repeatedly.

Ultimately the words we use and the way we communicate, regardless of specific language, always hold the capability to stand the test of time. Understand though, I use the phrase *"capability"* in this context carefully, given how often we waste our words and chances to connect with one another. When we actually commit to refining this, whether it's over the course of days or generations, our understanding of how we exist by ourselves *and* together becomes clearer. We become better at seeing the intangible atmospheres fostered between us and how they're inevitably connected to world events, thus appreciating how fundamental they are. It's through that endeavor to *articulate* more and more of who and what we are that we start to bring new phenomena of this life to light. In the long run, our outreach for compatibility will benefit when it comes to interacting as human beings. It's all an eternal domino effect giving birth to nuance. I guess you could say it's kind of cool.

Growth is an infinite endeavor in becoming the person you want to be throughout life

In the grand scheme of things, I actually believe that us human beings are far smarter than we give ourselves credit for at times (although I wholeheartedly admit I just misspelled 'smarter' while typing this, which is ironic I suppose.) But anyway, yes, the human race is usually far more inherently bright than we come off most of the time. *Most* of the time. This all in spite of the foolishness we've taken part in throughout our history. Trust me, it's often comical to actually sit and watch the news on television and see the incompetence we tend to partake in. Like, when I was a kid it was easy for me to question the common sense of those around me in addition to myself every now and then. What's interesting is realizing in hindsight how much of our intuition is built into us from the very beginning. A lot of times we just don't know how to interpret or use the knowledge we have about the world and ourselves in a meaningful manner before growing into adulthood.

I think it's fair to say when we're kids, we have an inherent ability to perceive certain elements of the environments around us. It's because of things like proven genetics and evolution that certain cognitive abilities persist through the generations, but on a deeper philosophical level, we don't know how to interpret that information during childhood. A lot of times we're unsure of how to best articulate our feelings and emotions in a variety of ways. For instance, I've been pretty reserved my whole life, but when I was a kid, and even a teenager, I really had no way of describing my personal desire for solitude at times. In my head, I was only able to refer to it as a feeling that was a deterrent for social interactions. I also could never really explain my perception of different social phenomena I saw while growing up despite understanding them. I think plenty of kids today have this sort of intuition, not just about their own lives, but of each other and the world around them as well. You know, the kind of instinct that gives us an inherent idea of what kind of world we're born into. On a biological level, that's how organisms work in the simplest way I'll admit, but I'm more so speaking on the ideas of purpose in life. We sometimes have inherent feelings on the meaning of things and what they imply. Even people who feel life has *no* meaning still deconstructed such an idea to an extent in order to subscribe to it. I feel to some degree that's based on intuition.

That instinct manifests differently between everyone however, allowing us to traverse this world in different ways. What I find interesting is how we ignore this within ourselves at times. It's kind of this situation where that knowledge in our minds sits in limbo at a young age. As we get older, we gain life experience and are able to connect the dots of what we see a lot more clearly. Take a stovetop for example. As a kid you're told not to touch the stove when it's hot. Why? Because it'll burn you and will hurt very badly. Most kids understand this concept, grasping the principle of action and consequence. They understand what happens when you touch a heated stovetop. Now take a kid of the same age, who say, was also taught this early on, yet decided to touch it anyway, only to fully realize the full severity of the consequences through being burned. Both children have knowledge on this matter, yet the former's is based on absorbing outside information, with the latter having experienced it firsthand. On paper, you could argue their understanding is on equal footing, however I'd point out that one of them has that experience more ingrained into them, resulting in a deeper understanding of the concept. This doesn't mean the second child is mentally superior, or more well off in life because of this. What it does mean however is that knowledge is often reinforced by experience in life. It makes what you already know that much more useful when nurtured by both the best and worst of life. It really goes back to the common discussion of knowledge vs wisdom to some regard. The difference lies in how you translate and apply knowledge to the reality around you, as well as to what degree. Despite all the gifts humankind has, plenty of us still fall short in this regard.

The same can even be said about this book for instance. I think deep down, a lot of what I've been discussing are things some people already see in life for themselves without me talking about them. But the experience of reading, and letting your psyche engage both with ideas you empathize and disagree with alike will *hopefully* reinforce some things in your mind. I mean, if I'm being honest, writing this has been an adventure in and of itself, making me really contemplate these topics more personally as I go about my own life, often being forced to live out what I write week by week. Simply put, gaining experience is eye opening, and it helps you begin to see not just how certain elements of life are interconnected like a puzzle, but how certain pieces fit in multiple places. The way I see it, that's what keeps life interesting despite its predictability at times. Moreover, it's about realizing by the end of your lifetime, you probably won't have all the pieces put together, but hopefully you can still see the big picture.

That being said, it's still worth refining who you are and what you stand for as a person *throughout* that lifetime, something that can't be stressed enough. Although, typically when you hear people talk about self-improvement, self-help, personal growth, whatever, it's basically always about becoming your best self and living your best life. Now both of those are sentiments I very much empathize with, especially given my own poor life choices, low self-esteem, and ignorance at times. But, what always kind of turns me off with that message isn't the moral itself, but rather the self-inflicting limits it places on you. In becoming your best self, you've reached the end of your transformation. You exist in your ideal state of being. It's the idea that your peak is already set in stone, a set point you choose, and you just have to rise up to it that I feel is misleading. My problem is simply that it's not true. When you contemplate your individual potential, it's very true that we all have limits, and to put it bluntly, things we will never be capable of achieving in our lifetimes, that's just fact. But what I see too often are people just aiming to reach that one single point to get the ultimate satisfaction, without really considering how far *beyond* those limits they could go. It's kind of like the problem with weight loss I've heard correctly pointed out; people will diet up until the point they achieve their ideal fitness, and then fall off course, thus regressing health wise. The diet isn't just a thing you do for a set time and then stop. Ideally, it should become a permanent improvement in your lifestyle. An everlasting refinement in the quality of your life. That doesn't mean you have to be a health freak forever or give up your affinity for comfort food. It means you *add on* to the things fostering longevity in your life. Dropping those ten pounds, or achieving that certain body aesthetic is great, but if you put the methods used to build up to those points on a shelf to be forgotten, it's only self-defeating in the long run.

This isn't to legitimize becoming obsessed with being better though. I say this as someone who's had to learn this the hard way. Regardless of my accomplishments, there were times in my life I was constantly driven not by motivation, but by the fear of never being good enough no matter how much work I put into myself or what I was doing. So of course, in trying to abide by my own advice, I got carried away with feeling that I had to surpass my limits, otherwise, what worth did I have? I eventually had to learn there's a balancing act when it comes to growth in life (which I admit sounds like a cop out at this point given how many times I've spoken on balance now). Truly it's an art to establish equilibrium within every corner of yourself and your life. Finding that balance first means taking pride in the new heights you manage to reach, even if they're small, daily wins. Believe me when I say letting an *unhealthy* desire for improvement fester undermines what you have to be confident about in yourself in the immediate present. In that scenario, all you can see is what you lack as opposed to what you've become.

At the end of the day, potential is a fine-tuned instrument sharpened from further use and dulls from lack of it. Like practicing with an instrument, giving yourself permission to build on what you can do little by little, day in and day out, without going overboard is how you make real progress on yourself. Even when you become old, withered, and your physical body fails you, there is no end to refining your existence. There is no end to working at becoming a better version of yourself, even through the many days filled with doubt, setbacks, and disappointments. Reaching for that growth in spite of all that and seeking to surpass who you were yesterday is an infinite endeavor that only stops when you stop. Whether that end is by death or by choice is up to you.

When we *do* die however, this experience isn't solely a result of your own chosen path in life. To be frank, we're always learning from others around us, and more importantly, the generations of people preceding *and* succeeding us. Whether it's to surpass the achievements of those before us, or mentor those we see a younger version of ourselves in, varying sources of knowledge to draw from exist in every corner of the universe, all interconnected in ways we don't always understand, but still have the option to make use of. Our intuition serves to tap into that when we stop and listen, both to ourselves, and each other's train of thought. In building on what you can do bit by bit, you start to realize just how helpful the right kind of people are in understanding those connections being woven around you. That's how you embrace such progress and experience without going crazy trying to grasp all of it on your own. You let other people help lift the burden off and do the same in return.

The life we share and live off from each other is what helps us grow into the best kind of people. It's a cycle that, even in the darkest moments of human history, has helped us advance beyond what our biology requires for survival. Obviously that's not something so easily measured by science, but I'd argue it's something intuitive among human beings nevertheless.

I learned what it truly means to be family after having mine annoy me for decades, just so I could write this for you. You're welcome.

When I was a kid, people used to complain that I never smiled. Looking back there were plenty of reasons for this, but honestly, I think I just didn't see any reason to, at least not all the time that is. That's not to say I was an unhappy child though. On the contrary, there were plenty of things that made me happy, but despite being the kid of a mother who typically wore her emotions on her sleeve, I was pretty much always the opposite, despite being an emotional person by nature myself. That combined with being so introverted made it easy for me to rarely express my feelings or true thoughts, often just being complicit with what others around me thought or felt, friends and family alike. Honestly though, if you've been reading along this far it should come as no surprise that I was a strange child growing up. I mean, I was the kid perfectly content in playing with rocks, sticks, and weeds by myself for hours at a time during summer for example. Actually, I still do really weird things to this day. For instance, I rarely ever put syrup on appropriate foods I'm eating like waffles and pancakes, and I'm very meticulous about the way I eat in general at times, often wanting to save the best part of the meal for last, so I'll purposefully eat around it. One specific thing I still do is always flipping a hamburger upside down after I take at least one bite of it, otherwise I feel uncomfortable. Another thing is I don't type properly on a keyboard at all. I learned how you're *supposed* to, but to this day I rapidly type using three fingers on my right hand, and just one on my left. I also use a steak knife to cut things you're *not* supposed to cut a steak knife with. It also shouldn't be a surprise that I don't hold a pencil correctly either, always placing one between my thumb and middle finger instead of index, and it's always been something that drives my mother insane. Truthfully, most of my family lineage are made up of weird people, so inheriting so many abnormal tendencies makes sense upon reflection, but even as a kid, I couldn't deny how much of a black sheep I was in relation to everyone else.

Reflecting on this as I got older was more of a subconscious pursuit however, though I admit it became more apparent during my teen years. It was a constant feeling of being an outsider even amongst my friends who grew to be family for me. Paradoxically, despite always feeling different, I grew a desire to make a difference in the world the more time I contemplated career paths. By then I had just started high school, but really didn't know where I wanted my life to go. All I knew is that I really wanted to help people in some way. I wanted nothing more than to change the world somehow. It's funny though because I think even back then I realized how cliche that ideal is in today's day and age. Realistically you can find anyone that *genuinely* wants to help people and make a difference no matter where you look, as well as hot takes on how the world *needs* to be changed. That's partially why I always had a hard time focusing on specific studies that would allow me to do that. I mean, if I was going to change the world, it should be by doing something unique to myself after all right? Despite this, it was often hard imagining I could live up to such an ideal while burdened with so many inadequacies both regarding my home life and entire being as a whole.

See, my immediate family consisted of myself, my younger brother, my mother (as my parents were divorced), and my grandparents. I wouldn't say we were dirt poor through my childhood and adolescence, but struggling to keep our heads above water financially was a consistent reality. Even though I was just a kid in reality, I absolutely hated not being able to do much to give my family a better life, and I hated not being able to provide for my mother. I remember I always dreamed of making enough money to put her in the nicest house I could buy someday, and all I wanted was to be able to tell her that everything was going to be okay during especially tough times. Yet simultaneously I struggled to believe that myself. These feelings would come to manifest in different ways as I got older, but I'd say the deepest sentiment was one of guilt over wanting to follow my own path in life despite our adverse lifestyle, for several reasons. Simply put, the reality that people like my brother and I were coming up in an era where societal thinking was shifting drastically began to set in over time, at times being at odds with the way we were raised, and our family history. I myself would often wonder if it was wrong for me to question my family's worldview on certain things despite wanting to take care of them.

On a broader level, coming to terms with my family's legacy while wanting to create my own was a tumultuous process over the years. As my desire to really be someone for others grew, the differences between me and my family resulted in more conflicting feelings. While I always wanted to provide for them, I also became privier to some of the underlying, darker dysfunction that existed. If I'm being blunt, I couldn't help but see so many toxic behaviors and mindsets on both sides of the tree by the time I reached adolescence. Character traits and attitudes that, as time went on, I realized were pretty messed up. Intense anger, being apathetic, passive aggressiveness, miscommunication issues, and even just being downright cold and spiteful all managed to persist through the generations. Whenever I thought of this, it was always easy to see those flaws in my own personality at times, manifested in darkness. I had my own capacity for unparalleled rage and apathy that reared its head at times. Although in my early teens I refused to admit this to myself, but I knew it on a subconscious level. I knew those traits were magnified in me and were just as toxic when I gave into them. Because of this, I hated being compared to certain people in my family, as it was a constant reminder that I was nothing more than an amalgam of everything wrong with my lineage. That at the end of the day, no matter how much of a difference I want to make in people's lives, I was just another damaged kid from a broken home, and to think I could ever be anything more than that was utterly pathetic. I hated feeling like this, and in turn hated feeling like I had no choice but to be the person my family expected me to be, because no matter how I looked at it, who I wanted to be wasn't just unattainable, but would never be good enough for the people I cared for. So I wanted nothing more than to reject so much of what I inherited in the way of personality traits. Reject even the idea that I was anything like what I had grown to detest. But deep down, I was also so afraid that somewhere along the line I would lose my way in life.

Ironically, it wasn't until I got older did I see that in my attempt to rebuke that legacy was exactly what held me back from making peace with it in order to move forward. I grew to understand this little by little as I got older, but I think it was most apparent by the time I hit my early twenties. By then, three out of four of my grandparents had passed away, and to say their impacts hit hard would be an understatement. Those years saw much change in the world, and I had endured and bore witness to much death, poverty, mental illness—even homesickness was a recurring theme through my travels. I spent plenty of time in dark places from being depressed to having mental breakdowns, to just being completely burned out mentally, spirituality, and emotionally. Incidentally you'll find the temptation to be cynical grows with resentment over life's misfortunes, and there was no shortage of that. Nevertheless, even as a child I always took immense pride in my own willpower to deal with such rough periods, yet there's no denying a major reason I never gave into those darker emotions was due to having people in my life who brought out the best in me. Friends outside of family, who ironically deserve to be branded with that status. In nature I've always been stubborn, and prideful over being able to hold it all together amid any of life's adversities regardless of difficulty or pain, or pressure, yet it's always been at my lowest point that I've had to admit I can only get so far on my own with that mindset. The nuance between being someone who endures that darkness versus someone who overcomes it depends on the people you let into your life. I contemplated this as I traveled and met more people who would become significant parts of my life in ways I never expected or asked for. At some point I saw the irony in creating a life for myself as the generations before me lost theirs was unmistakably apparent. As the one to succeed them, I began to reevaluate not just their lives, but people like my parents as well, and everyone else who had come before me. It was a matter of seeing that at times I was so focused on not losing my way or continuing the dysfunction of my family, that I forgot about so much of the good things my family emulated for each other and as people. Truthfully I can think back and recall the most severe, hurtful arguments between some of us. Such deplorable words, actions, and lack of support for one another were all weighted reasons I had to be cold and resentful. Yet at the same time, I couldn't keep ignoring every reason I had not to give up on those very people because of how much I care for them. That in spite of everything we had been through as a family, mine still had the ability to be the best kind of people when it truly counted. In trying to completely distance myself from the idea I could perpetuate what ran in my blood, I ignored all the ways I was exactly like other relatives. I had to learn to be at peace with how I'm just like my parents for instance, because it was people like them who built their lives in a way where I could choose for myself what kind of man and person I want to be. People like my mother who I was closest to at times sacrificed so much without any recognition or reward so I could have the choice of being better than much of the darkness we had all grown to acknowledge existed at times.

Honestly, I wasn't an easy child to raise by *any* stretch of the imagination. In the grand scheme of things, my mom couldn't always give me the life I wanted, but she gave me the life I needed to become the person I am today, and that's a debt I can never fully repay to her. Finding peace in that is understanding that what's passed onto you is yours, and yours alone, regardless of how much you may want to reject or ignore it. All you can do with that is embrace it as your own and improve on it. It's realizing that what's inside isn't a sole reflection of where you come from, but rather a tool to decide what you'll become in this life. That's an integral part of deciding who to be. You're not bound by your lineage, but it is up to you to decide whether to break the cycle of what you want to change, or perpetuate it.

Accepting this and seeing there was more to the reality I was living kept me contemplating these kinds of bonds we have with people, mainly during instances where I was furthest from home and family. I mentioned before being introverted can be a double-edged sword when desiring meaningful interactions but also isolation, and this was something that really set in during periods of homesickness and genuine loneliness. Wanting to change the world, and in working to educate myself on everything in it led to some of the most memorable adventures in my life, yet part of that always meant those stories come to an end eventually. At some point or another you have to part ways with the people walking a similar path beside you, and going from one journey in life to the next often leaves you with nostalgia over what's left behind. Regardless of whether you're lonely or not, you have a lot of time to think about this when you spend hours alone on planes, buses, in airports, on boats, in hostels, etc., and it really makes you reflect on certain relationships you have with individual people in your life or circle, and what they mean to you. It's not just the nostalgia over the good times that hits you, but also the lessons that came out of the worst times. It makes you reevaluate what connections with those people persist even in their absence, because the hard truth is, not all of them last. It's really no secret, but not everyone is meant to stay in your life long term, and that goes for friends and relatives alike. Despite that, I've found it's often the people most willing to reconnect with each other in a *healthy* manner that prove to be true family to one another. As time goes on, most people change and reinvent themselves in some way, and the attachment you might have with someone may be from days long gone. Distance develops even in the best of friendships, and sometimes people grow apart one way or another. But I truly believe that it's the people you're willing to find your way back to that make up your real family in life, blood or not. Regardless of how long it's been, regardless of the constant lifestyle changes and distance life puts between you, it's those people you know in your heart you'll always come home to, one way or another that are your real family. It's those bonds which transcends such distance that lay at the root of this social group we call "family."

In my own experience that's come with the challenge of filtering out those kinds of people from others who were admittedly a bad influence on my life. At times that was a matter of acknowledging my *own* intuition about toxic people, and in others it was a matter of seeing who's brought out the best in who I am. In the same way I've learned not to give up on other people, I also realized how many people I have in my life who never gave up on me as well, even during times where

I felt I didn't deserve such kindness. It's been through that I've seen the value in not giving up on yourself either. Through the times you spend laughing with loved ones over the dumb inside jokes together or having the deepest conversations on the most random nights. Those are the meaningful connections that help put life into perspective. Those are the motivations behind starting new, healthier cycles after you've broken toxic ones.

When I think about the direction of my life story, I'm reminded that it doesn't belong to me alone. My chosen path, and my desire to make a difference can't be embodied by what I alone see in this world, not when a huge part of it is seeing the role I play in every life that crosses my path while I'm alive. At the end of the day, the imprint you leave on those people long outlives you once you've left this physical world. That's how you write your own legacy. You try your hardest to manifest that vision into something which transcends you and can inspire other people to do the same long after you're gone from this world. In striving to do that, you realize those who remind you of how much you have to lose are also the ones who leave you with everything to live for. So carry that with you through the story of your life, using it as reason to smile in the face of what threatens to hold you back in it.

A commentary on religion from an unconventional Christian

Well, I guess I was bound to get deep into more controversial stuff sooner or later right? Although to be fair, It's really no secret the mysticism around higher powers and omniscient being is a point of contention among people, often to the point where, like politics, some won't even bother bringing it up because of how divisive religion can be at times. Still, I honestly think it can be one of the most fascinating things to study if you can look at things secularly.

For one thing, I find it intriguing how religion and belief are two different things in hindsight. I mean, all religions and the practices that go with them are man-made social systems when you *really* break them down. Of the various faith's people follow in this world, they all claim to know the way toward an ideal existence, both for the individual, and collectively. Now, I know there's nuance that goes with such a statement given the *complexities* of different faiths, but generally speaking, they all offer guidelines to being a good person and living a good life. That common theme leads every religion to offer an explanation for the layers of reality that surrounds us. They offer an answer for the eternal question of 'why' that's tied to existence itself. Moreover, the reasoning behind those explanations ultimately derives from mortal interpretation, which I think is important to acknowledge when looking at the influence it has on humanity. From the start of our history, we've always sought to make sense of what's greater than us after all. At its core though, why you should live your life in a given way, or why a deity wants you to live a certain way, is rooted in human perception of what may lie beyond us. The smallest rituals, such as prayer, worship and the proper way to do it are dictated by what human beings deem as meaningful and essential to life, regardless of whether it's posed as a message from a higher power. The same goes for the creation and preservation of religious texts as well. It's no secret that figures in history have added or removed things at their personal discretion when it's come to literature, ultimately shifting how writings were translated and passed down.

Belief on the other hand isn't limited to rules or rituals in the same manner, often encompassed more by personal experience and intuition. However, it *is* influenced by social realities in a similar manner to entire religious systems. Most of such discussion starts with the question of if there's a higher power or not. Is there a God? What people overlook is how, despite contemplating if an objective answer exists, the mere presence of the question seems to already confirm it. What I mean is, human beings, regardless of whatever spiritual experiences, awakenings etc., that we claim to have, are the end interpreters for what kind of entity a God would be. *Generally* speaking, we characterize God as one of absolute knowledge, power, and ability. Honestly just thinking about this reminds me of an old stupid query posed to me once, which basically asked, "Can God create a burrito so hot that even he can't eat it?" If the answer is "yes," that's a problem, because God can't eat the burrito, which means God, who is supposed to be able to do anything, can't do something. Likewise, if the answer is "no," then God can't create such a burrito, also meaning he can't do something. The more you think about it, the more you realize it creates a paradox, however it also serves as one perfect example for how humans create and confirm the existence of God and his qualities. Such a paradox shows the assumption that God exhibits human characteristics and behaviors. Perfect evidence is referring to God with the pronoun, "he," like I'm doing right now. Really, I think this derives from the mindset that God created human beings in his image. With that narrative in mind, we often look at God in *our ever-changing* image. We attribute God with mortal traits and abilities like being happy, angry, jealous, etc., and acting on those traits in his own divine manner all the time really. Some of the greatest evidence of this is probably all the religious artwork that's been produced for centuries. So when you ask if God exists, humanity has spent a good chunk of our existence painting a picture, quite literally and figuratively, of what kind of entity God truly is, and those interpretations and stories have influenced the world almost to the degree of which some will claim God has in his own right. It's also worth noting I'm not just looking at this from a monotheistic, Christian perspective. This all applies to other religions in the sense that we personify godhood. Regardless of the nuance in qualities to different divine figures, either human qualities are attributed to the depiction of gods, or divine qualities are scaled to the level of significant people in religious history, like with divine monarchies for example. In any case, what exists beyond us as divine and godlike is constructed in our human image. Our inherent physical, psychological, and spiritual capabilities for the essence of creation, and to recognize creation, is what gives way to this. I also think it influences how we perceive the concept of prophecy when you think about it. In some sense I'd argue things like scripture, proverbs, etc., are a variation of what I spoke on earlier; our ability to predict the future. This considering how many people take such literature as a sign for what's to come in life, an omen so to speak. Strangely enough I think it's also a matter of superstition. Like if someone says misfortune will befall you for doing what they consider wrong or sinful, and then repeated bad breaks start happening, you'd be surprised how many people freak out and wonder if there's some truth to it. I mean, realistically there's a ton of movies and TV shows showing this trope, but people tend to give power to that kind of foresight in real life as well. Although I'll admit I'm actually pretty superstitious and see validity in omens myself, so I'd be lying if I said I've never bought into that kind of thinking.

All that being said, I don't think it's a stretch to say we've not only used, but *refined* these abilities throughout history, both in secular living and religion. I'd argue our interpretation of who/what God is, and what is god-like per se, is constantly evolving across time and space. What we acknowledge as possibilities for reality under the jurisdiction of absolute power and creation constantly changes. Now, this may be a bit of a tangent, but that idea is why I find people with god-complexes to be so interesting. It's because their self-image doesn't seem to be rooted in mere superiority, but rather a true belief that their existence is far above the limitations of humankind altogether. In describing themself as a god, they internalize the question,

"What other word is there to describe me?" "Delusional" works pretty well, but that's beside the point. While that's obviously a radical state of mind, I do think to some degree, human beings naturally want to be as close to godhood as possible while retaining what uniquely makes us human. Understand when I say this, I'm really talking in the broadest of terms with the word "godhood." My opinion on that isn't as profound as I'm making it seem. I just think an underlying desire to control the boundaries of what we are in life is inherent in different social groups among us.

Now, I know I kind of already spoke on being limitless as a person, advocating for it even, but I think it's also important to understand while such mindsets are capable of elevating us, they can also be toxic when they breed superiority. I think such phenomena reveal itself in different social systems among people, as well as the levels that distinguish them. Take the various positions in the workplace for instance. Plenty of us have observed or dealt firsthand with a boss or coworker that's just too arrogant about their job. Whether we're talking about the CEO of the biggest company in the world, or the principle of a random elementary school, we've all known those that take a *little* too much pride in their place at the top. The same idea goes for simple group dynamics when someone stays adamant about being in charge or the overseer of everything. Regardless of the social scale, the pride we sometimes take in our hierarchical status can become toxic. Toxic to the point that we'll put down others so that our own authority is absolute. I think a reason for this is because in order to *make* that status absolute and meaningful, the validation brought from it must also be absolute, so why not embrace that authoritative power to do so? Again, I don't think that's inherently bad when it comes to human nature, just dangerous when people run away with that power, even on the smallest of levels.

Similar to what I was saying earlier though, these tendencies help influence how we approach ideas of higher existence and creation. In my own life, I was raised as a Christian, and still identity as one. Yet over time, I've had to constantly reevaluate how I embrace my own religion the more and more I experience what this life has to offer. Looking back, I'd actually say I had a pretty general upbringing when it came to being taught about God, church, etc. Honestly, I always took those teachings at face value for years, never really questioning my own beliefs or values until I got older. It was a gradual process when it came to examining my own way of thinking, but it was also a reluctant one as well. I think sometimes people view questioning one's beliefs or religion to mean you're devoid of faith, or even fear you're going down a dark path, and because of that I always had a reluctance to embrace different ideas that didn't seem compatible with Christianity. I remember learning about existential nihilism as a teenager, which basically (and it can get complicated the deeper into it you get) asserts that there is no inherent meaning to life or existence itself. There is no predestined fate, no higher power guiding and protecting you, nor things like signs hinting at what to do next in life. I disagreed with some of the general tenets, but also saw the validity of others comprising that train of thought. At the time learning about it took me for a loop considering how so much of my beliefs seemed to be upended in the face of this other ideology. Ironically, it came from trying to think critically about so many different philosophies in the long run that I realized; doubting your own ideas and values is actually quite the opposite of losing faith. When it comes to beliefs and values that ultimately determine your lifestyle and worldview, it's important to play devil's advocate with yourself and be able to *deeply* question *why* you choose to believe in certain things. Look close enough, and you'll see plenty of people who only abide by certain morals and standards not because they personally *believe* in them, but because it's what their religion requires. Their religion says they'll be rewarded if they act *this* way and punished should they act *that* way. Some people live a certain way because it's just how they were raised, or just how they're inner circle approves of them. To be fair though, on a wide scale you could *certainly* make the argument that such practice is more beneficial to humanity than damaging. So long as groups of people treat each other kindly and ensure social stability, why does it matter if they're only doing it for a reward? Honestly, there's merit in that idea, but at the end of the day it's...disingenuous. It becomes this thing where your standard for morality is superficial, yet plenty will take the moral high ground despite it, and I can honestly say I've seen this manifest in plenty of people. The truth is you won't get anywhere unless you can handle delving into ideas and mindsets that spit in the face of your initial views. Sometimes it means being willing to upend your own worldview in order to broaden it and revamping your entire thought process to better understand the many layers to reality, not just the one you understand best.

Reflecting on this through my teen years helped me see my earlier point of changing views for what God is, as I really think it's been a slow generational shift. People have grown to doubt older, more traditional approaches toward religion and belief, often in favor of more varied, existential perspectives in. Of course, when you remember there are still people who embrace a sense of spirituality and faith, going through life while exposed to such contradictory ideas can make you question if there even is a "right path." To put it bluntly, I don't really think there is. I don't think there's one *best* way to explain existence or how to thrive in it. As I got older and understood this, I realized that If I was to identify as a Christian, I didn't want it to be because I grew up as one and knew nothing else, but rather because I chose to be one. Even then, I've always somewhat perceived myself as being unconventional as a Christian due to how abstract my own subjective view of reality can be at times. By that I mean I don't perceive my own faith or connection to Christianity, as strong as it might be, as the only valid explanation for how life or the universe fully works. Simply put, you could read the Bible, or any religious literature really, from cover to cover and you still won't have all the answers to life we often seek. No one religion or ideology alone gives a full picture of reality.

If anything, I think many disciplines have overlapping ideas people often ignore, the most general of which actually characterizes the inherent duality of human existence itself: light and darkness, two essences representing opposite ends of a spectrum. Plenty of social theories, philosophies, religions, etc., constantly echo concepts of light and darkness in people and life, albeit they're articulated and labeled in differing ways. In some cases they're described as order and chaos, or grace and suffering, or beauty and tragedy for instance. You could make the argument these are all separate concepts in their own right, but I think they're all treated with the same sentiment in relation to people when we get introspective. One is ideal, the other should be avoided. One helps us find peace in life, and the other leads us to feeling lost and broken at times. Yet somewhere in between is a balanced existence. Where that balance *is* though has always been a point of contention amongst humanity. I think different religions and the philosophies they introduce seek to cover as much of that spectrum as possible, with some covering ideas from one end more than others. They provide us with stories, imagery, and music that, even if you're not religious, aid in how we contemplate that reality in between. Those kinds of deeper lessons that may initially come off as high and mighty somehow always manage to echo through time. The simplest examples being how we encourage each other to practice kindness, don't run away with your anger, don't be greedy for material things, etc. They all play out repeatedly in modern society. Take the discouragement to murder for instance, less you corrupt yourself and hurt others. Even with a secular mindset, most people would agree there's some general truth from religious suggestions for how to get along with others, this despite our nature of conflict with one another. If you pay attention, you'll find there are more than one valid suggestion for how humans should live in peace. like I said, looking at the perspective of just one doesn't give a full picture of existence, but rather just a small glimpse into the realm of possible answers.

Don't get me wrong though, a multireligious perspective doesn't mean you have to structure your life around every applicable life philosophy. It's just the willingness to look at other branches of thinking, even when contradictory to one another, that helps us think critically in the simplest ways about life. It helps to see how differing theories on life and the universe can be put together. There is no one definitive answer for the question of existence, rather there are multiple correct answers, each branching out to their own implications for reality. It's kind of like if you were to look at multi-dimensional painting for example. If you isolate one given section from the frame, it may start to appear as a separate image in and of itself, and while beautiful in its own right, if you extend your view outwards, you'll see it's just part of an even greater narrative.

All that being said, such pieces of a greater narrative permeate their way into even the most secular of values in any society. Sometimes it's for the better, other times for the worst. But regardless of if you personally have no use for religion, spirituality, etc., there is no denying that even in the most fact-based reality of our physical makeup, we're inherently connected to the rest of the universe. Despite how small and seemingly insignificant we are, we exist as a force of nature in this reality, often seeing the duality of who and what we are continue to play out across millennia. Essences akin to light and darkness can almost never exist without the other, and if they do, it's only for a short time. That's why there is no such thing as a *true* utopia despite humanity's historic efforts to create one, nor a *true dystopia*, at least not as we'd imagine it. A vision of both ends up manifesting as one in reality, and as a result, we live in a world that's kind in some ways and horrifically cruel in others. As a result, its led us to deeply think about our purpose and the variables around it, often embracing things like imagery of the hero or saviors for instance. In our best stories, music, and fantasies it makes us question ourselves; What do you see in humanity that's worth saving? What's forever interesting is the many beautiful answers created by many beautiful people. In my personal opinion, I've grown to believe humanity is God's longest short story that's still being written, but of course that's just one way of looking at things. Ultimately, despite the abundance of moral subjectivity and even *inconsistency* at times, religion, God, and spirituality is always going to prove a useful frame of thought for humanity, even if how it's embraced is reinvented.

Can humans truly evolve?

By this point I think it's well established human beings are pretty interesting creatures. we're not the only sentient species living on this grand planet, but for now at least, we're the greatest interpreters of life and existence. Granted, that's an ironic statement considering how young we are compared to the rest of the universe, and that's *including* how far back our homo subspecies go in terms of evolution. The thousands of years humans have thrived are really just a brief moment alongside the eons passed since the formation of the cosmos. When I think of this, I wonder what humanity's true potential is given how new we are at being conscious in general. The accomplishments we've made in the past thousand, or even just hundred years are astounding when you take the fragility of human life into account. And yet, I feel there are so many other flaws within our nature as people that still hold us back at times and it begs the question: in the grand scheme of our time in this universe, can we ever *truly* evolve beyond our inherent weaknesses and imperfections, or are destined to always fall back I to patterns of our default nature?

    I'm not asking in the raw biological sense, but rather in the way of consciousness, sentience, and what's considered humane in life, although I concede that *can* be linked to science depending on how you look at it, i.e. raw psychology, natural chemicals in humans, hormones, etc. Often we act like our advancements have led us on an upward, linear climb in how we embrace morality, ethics, civil society/makeup, heck, even just general common sense among people. We've made so much progress in just *existing* plainly as a species, that along the way, many advancements have seen us deviate from our natural instincts as people. Earlier I spoke on technology influencing our development, yet I also wonder if any of that matters in the long run when it comes to the *root* of our existence in this universe. So much of our being is still incompatible with our own creations to be frank. Simple things like sitting in front of higher and higher resolution screens each year, obsessing over social metrics like followers and influencers, or even more economic things like sitting in an office all day that fosters no *real* motivation but is good for generating money in society. These things aren't *inherently* unhealthy or a vice to the world, but sooner or later we somehow always embrace them to our detriment. So I ask, that despite the progress we've made over thousands of years, is it really enough to say we've become elevated as a sentient species within the universe? Or will we always be subject to our human defects?

Oddly enough, I think I first started asking myself this through watching the Walking Dead as a teenager. As nerdy as it may sound, the concept of a world where an apocalyptic virus breaks down society to nothing intrigued me from a philosophical standpoint. The depiction of certain shifts in human behavior during disaster situations, and the depiction of humanity's descent into savagery and brutality were themes I couldn't help but analyze myself. Of course, there are plenty of other shows and movies that pose their own variations of such "what if?" tales. Through all of them we get these dystopian realities devoid of sustainable order, often asking the question of how easily are you willing to compromise your morals and higher values just to survive. How willing are you to embrace your most primal instincts despite how civilized your noblest ideals were, or rather, how *quickly* will you embrace them, as a survival of the fittest world is often portrayed as demanding as much in order to adapt. Things like murder, stealing, looting, exploiting and manipulating people for protection or resources, or even just abandoning others to save yourself. I think it's a worthy question to ask when contemplating the breakdown of society in a true crisis scenario. Now of course depending how into those kinds of stories you are, we could debate plenty of problems and impracticalities with certain world depictions, but that's not the point here, the point is as a long standing theme in fiction, we often look at the actions of desperate humans and take the moral high ground of, "Oh I would never act like that, go that far, be that brutal, etc." Even when we acknowledge there will always be a percentage of people who adopt truly callous survival tactics, we usually imagine ourselves as being the outliers in these bleak fantasy situations, myself included. You'd like to imagine if it were down to you and someone else with not enough resources to stay alive much longer, you wouldn't beat them to death just to save yourself. You'd at least *try* to find a way to save both of you. Or at the *very* least, admit that you'd look out for you and what's yours, but feel bad about having to do so...but would you really? If it were someone who let's say once posed a threat to your survival or your survivor group, would their loss *really* eat at you if you knew they were a liability?

Don't get me wrong though, the most callous parts of human nature aren't *always* inherent for the sole reason of showing us what behavior is immoral. Considering how the world has legitimately resembled barbaric wastelands at various points in time, to be less than empathetic to everyone in your path wasn't an abnormal thing. To be selfish in some respects taught self-preservation. To know cruelty teaches how to avoid being taken advantage of. Arrogance has produced unparalleled ambition for humans to one up and compete with each other, leading to plenty of innovations, even if it has been the downfall of many. In the end, simple ignorance about life, the world, and the universe, despite how destructive it may be, is a prerequisite for humanity to ascend.

The fact of the matter is, these are character traits that have always played a role in getting humanity to a place where we don't *need* them as intensely. Many of our ancestors wanted a world where you can afford to share freely with one another, and not constantly look over your shoulder from paranoia. A world where civil cooperation is broadened on a far more global scale, and where people choose to show mercy during physical confrontation for instance. But as ideal as those preceding visions were, that's not how the world works in a lot of ways. For as far as we've come in the way of moral and ethical advancement, those millennia old behaviors are still hard wired into who we are as people, they just take on different forms at times. The global standard for selfishness is no longer hoarding the last piece of food when you and someone else are starving to death, but it *is* finding a legal loophole to steal people's money through your shady company. The global standard for cruelty is no longer having a public execution in order to strike fear in a people to act how you want, but rather ruining someone's reputation through everything from blackmail to canceling them online. The global standard for brutality is no longer just beating the life out of someone that challenges your authority, but has been refined through the existence of organized crime, which I guess still constitutes beating the life out of someone depending on what *kind* of crime we're talking about, but you get the point. So *all that* being said, we still act and treat each other like trash a lot of the time despite how enlightened and woke we often pretend to be, even if it's not always on the level of literal life and death. Although, you *do* have to acknowledge how many parts of the world are still characterized by the more intense manifestations of what I've listed, like third world countries obviously. But across the board, time has shown us greater possibilities. Regardless, when you really think about it, our default, primal instincts are still a part of who we are, even when we deny it. They just conform to the time period we're living in. In many ways, we're a unique kind of animal still in the stages of infancy.

So if that's the case, what's to say that one day our current structures for civilization fail and we regress back to a more primal state of being? It sounds crazy, but pointing out that a world power like the United States is only a little over 200 years old in comparison to known, ancient civilizations that prospered *far* longer before their downfall is a legitimate example. Ones like the Mayan and Roman empire are popular examples. The same goes for other countries and nations in modern day, as plenty of societies we've built up over the past few centuries are young and fragile enough to fail from the simplest of mistakes.

It's not so much we haven't risen above our nature as it is that we've only *started* to as a species. We like to think that because we promote civil discourse (among plenty of other things) that we're so much more humane than a picture of humanity where everything from death to discrimination was a common occurrence, yet I don't think we're that far off in hindsight. At the same time though, I don't think that's something to feel hopeless over, nor is it a sign that everything built over the past few centuries is meaningless or fraught. On the contrary. What I've stressed like a broken record through this book is that the world, and what it means to be human is changing. The exponential advancements to life and how we perceive them are, up close, a phenomenon that makes us feel more than elevated from the likes of the past two or three generations even. But in reality, humanity has only just gotten started in its ascension as a sentient species. We're at a point where, because of things like technology, higher self-awareness, higher education in *so* many topics like politics, mental health, etc., and just our ability to imagine far more expansive simulations, we can choose to defy our nature in ways that are revolutionizing how we exist. If you're a 6ft tall behemoth of a man with insane athletic ability, you have the option of becoming a painter instead of a soldier per se because, deep down, you really don't like violence or conflict. Vice versa, if you're the shortest, skinniest person in the room who actually likes to fight, odds are there's a gym somewhere for you to learn how to box and compete in a smaller weight class. The thing is, for as much potential as we're starting to realize because of our failures and mistakes, it can still all go to hell just as easily because of the ones we make today. That's the double-edged sword of humanity. That's the risk we've been running since day one. You'll find that in the many experiments we conduct to make the world better, there is no do over option in any of them. When we mess up, whether it's the rules of a small town, or International policy, people's lives are affected in ways you have to live with into the future. Sooner or later we reap the consequences of our actions as people, regardless of the severity.

With this in mind, I think the question of whether we can truly evolve is a simultaneous yes and no. Imperfection and human defect will always help define humanity, it's a necessary evil to our entire existence in fact. Yet what allows us to progress in spite of that is the option to become something more than those darker moral impulses. Truthfully, I think that's something everyone is capable of on many levels. Scientific consensus asserts that the human race shares approximately 99.9% of the same DNA structure, leaving 0.1% of yourself that exists uniquely within this world. Considering how easy it is to see how many colorful differences we express, it should also be clear that such a small difference is all it takes to produce such beautiful variance throughout people in our world. The same principle holds true in a philosophical sense when we get in our introspective moods I'd say. Finding that slight deviation between not just you and everyone else, but everyone who came before, is all it takes to nurture your potential in this one, short, blink of a lifetime we have as a part of this universe. I think when everyone pursues to do that on an individual level, it resonates on the larger scale. That's how you end up with brilliant minds working together to innovate when the probability of them meeting was slim to none. I think that's part of what it means to become something more.

In the end, the progression of shaping who and what we are is an immensely slow burn in the context of this vast universe. After all, they say life is a marathon and not a sprint. The thing that gives us hope I feel, is being able to acknowledge we're picking up the pace. Don't get me wrong though, it isn't *so* imperative that everyone views it that deep, but that's yet another paradox of this world. Despite how complicated this world and its inhabitants are, I believe one of the meanings of this life is to simplify it as best we can, no matter which way we move forward.

An infinite cycle of death and rebirth is what colors in the circle of life

Death. It's an interesting word we have to describe something that moves out of existence...or at the very least reforms into something unrecognizable. I say this because we don't attribute death exclusively to living things, but rather to just "things" in general. As a result of this, there are many different layers to the term that present their own separate experiences in our lives. The physical death of people of course, but also, the metaphorical or philosophical death of self, the social death of a relationship, the death of an era, or even something more rigid like the death of a company as it goes out of business. Regardless of what it is, everything on every level runs its course in this world. Everything from the physical buildings that make up cities to the people in them is undeniably finite.

Of course, what we're arguably *most* intimate with is death between living things. I mean, it's no secret we interact with it as an entity unto itself, the entire depiction of the grim reaper in various art forms is proof of this. Even so, depictions of the lack of life essence take on endless forms through time, and again, that's just relating to the death of organisms first and foremost.

It affects us profusely. As it should.

Coincidentally while fearing it, we're also given an opportunity to find out how special our own mortality is in life. For now, this world serves as the only plane of existence we know of where we can experience meaningful sentience, and putting a time limit on that inherently influences how we embrace said experience. Now of course, there's always been plenty of beliefs and interpretations of an afterlife, along with the straight up denial of one as well. Some people see this world as a means to a greater one. Some think this life is the only life we're allotted. Others believe in something in between for their own reasons. Personally, I believe there's a distinction between our physical and spiritual selves that plays out across our time on this physical earth. The various stages in our lives, at one point or another, force us to question whether there truly is a spirit to our finite endeavors. Whether or not there's actually a *soul* behind the default psychological habits we exhibit. In my case, I've often pondered how feasible it is to say that we experience a spiritual, or internal death before we do in the physical sense.

I mean, of course there are plenty of religious answers, but I'll admit one thought experiment that's provoked me is actually the Ship of Theseus Paradox. If you don't know (and without getting into a history lesson) the Ship of Theseus paradox basically poses the question of whether or not you're still *you* after so much reinvention through life. Imagine you have a ship, except little by little, bit by bit, you replace different components of it with new, better ones, for whatever reason. At some point the gradual revamping of said ship forces the question of whether it's still the *original* ship you started with, or an entirely new one. One on hand, if the ship is unrecognizable from when you started, then the answer is 'of course' right? If everything from the exterior down to the bathrooms are replaced sooner or later, and especially if the functionality or performance changes, how is that not an entirely different vessel than what you started with? I think the same could be said about other things we engage with as well, like a car, or even a renovated house.

To build off of that, doesn't the same principle apply to human beings as well? We're engaged in a natural state of growth, maturity, and slow decline before eventually reaching death. At some point or another most of our *own* components are completely replaced as well. Regardless, I feel there's a discrepancy between applying this idea to people versus tangible objects. It's different for living beings as opposed to material items simply put. Unlike inanimate objects, humans are sentient beings striving to transform and be better over time. Yet even with that in mind, it still doesn't prove the person you are today is the same as who you were as a three-year-old. You could very well make an argument that despite a three-year-old you *growing into* the person you are now, they're still two completely different beings in their own right. I mean, how much do you *really* remember from that time?

Our mental faculties, flesh, bones, organs, cells, even bacteria—they all get replaced at one point or another. True not all at the same time, but eventually they all do for our sake of functionality as organisms. So under that reasoning, aren't we all dead to some degree when looking at ourselves in the past? Isn't it fair to say it's natural to lose ourselves in the stands of time? To say you've already died several times over? I think the solution to this is often taken for granted, and it's that we live as many different versions of our own selves throughout a lifetime. No one stays the same forever, and if they did, well that'd be pretty boring honestly. Who and what you were as a five-year-old, fifteen-year-old, and 25-year-old are all just different versions of oneself, tethered to the same, single line of consciousness.

The reason it's fair to say you are in fact the same sentient being, despite whatever metamorphosis you've undergone, is because that single line of existence in your lifetime is in fact the linchpin of it all. It's The fact that at the end of the day, it's *your life* to be experienced through *one*, and only one stream of existence in this universe.

That being said, I do think we all run the risk of experiencing a *true* death of self in life. I think in spite of all our untapped potential, our natural limitations still leave us open to the possibilities of being fully corrupted, even *with* being tethered to one life. There's a fine line to cross before someone becomes irredeemable, and yet I don't believe there to be only one answer for what it is, nor does it look the same for everyone either. Being corrupted doesn't always appear like Anakin Skywalker after he joined the dark side after all. It doesn't necessarily mean one is now "evil" per se or has done anything morally wrong. Rather it's when they manifest into nothing greater than their primal instinct, however they may show up in their environment, and cease trying to do so. A permanent sense of "stagnation" if you will.

What's interesting is I actually feel that most of us know this already. We feel it as we adapt to new challenges while still *attempting* to grow from them. We just don't always want to consciously acknowledge it. Sometimes we *feel* dead inside. Sometimes we go through and experience things that change us so radically, we don't even recognize ourselves anymore. We question whether or not we're too far gone from a version of ourselves we once knew...and in turn we question if the same can be said about the world we live in.

The death and reinvention of all that you are exists through one lifetime. It repeats itself throughout the different stages and phases we're immersed in. The day you think you're at peace with yourself and everything you are, cherish it. Hold onto it. Remember it. Because odds are something will come along one day and take you out of it. Something that really will threaten to kill you inside. Maybe it'll just be the inevitable changes to life. Or perhaps it will be the physical death of a loved one that traps you in a headspace of grief. By nature times of peace and tranquility are meant to be put in jeopardy, but that doesn't mean it's worth being paranoid or angst over.

Truth be told I've thought of this in regard to myself at times. One of the things I got set on when I was younger is the goal to live to see 100. You know, a cool checkpoint to say I reached in my lifetime, especially when I acknowledged how hereditary health problems ran in my family as I got older. Yet I also saw how bittersweet it may end up being considering that living such a long life ultimately means *outliving* so much of the greatest things that define it. Friends, family, heck even reruns of TV shows, stores going out of business, restaurant menu changes, etc. With that comes the same cycle of grief and loss over and over and over again. I've legitimately wondered if I'll be tainted by that pain to the point where I'm too tired of living to enjoy it anymore.

But, as opposite as it may sound, that's not always a bad thing. In the same way times of peace and tranquility run their course, both inside of us and our societies, so do times of adversity and painful transition. Everything dies. Everything *will* die. What's material will Inevitably deteriorate. Your home, and every item in it you're emotionally attached to will wither away someday, regardless of who it's passed down to or how many times. Your pets will eventually die. Every relationship will meet its last hug, smile, and goodbye someday. Eras end. Dynasty's end. And even the greatest of generations are eventually laid to rest. Sooner or later everything runs its course, not *just* in life or in this world, but among existence itself. Someday our sun will burn out and will probably destroy our entire planet as a result. Whether life still persists on earth by then or has moved on really doesn't matter. At some point all life in the universe will cease to exist because, well, even this *universe* will cease to exist. Whether it's by heat death or one of the many other theories for its demise, this universe will die by the end of its *own* clock, at least as we conventionally know it that is. The many stars and constellations we've grown fond of, the ones we've stared at while having deep conversations with our loved ones were always destined to part ways with us.

And it is sad. It's very sad.

But I think the fact that we feel this about so many things, the fact that we question how to go on is a testament to how much of a purpose they serve in the grand scheme of things. The answer when asking where eternity and infinity fit into this is, everything begins anew. Every birth and every start comes off the tails of a predecessor. A previous story. A precursor to a given reality. This cycle persists infinitely on every level.

Live long enough and you'll see that cycle at work in small, interesting ways. A child going on a similar journey of self-discovery similar to one you've seen before for instance. Or a promising new society/social structure growing in the place where an old great fell. Or a revolution composed of minds that see themselves as the first of their kind. Live long enough and you begin to see this cycle turn into different shades of different colors, but the wheel always comes back around.

In truth, it's easy to become fatigued from being attached to the best of it, only to have to let go once more eventually. And yet, every story that ends, and every stage of grief we endure ironically offers us a chance to be at peace with what we've experienced. To take that time, however short it may have been, or however *unfair* or *unjust* and find peace with what it taught us. Peace in what it's *shown* us about living in *this* universe, because I do think the universe itself will start again at some point, just not in a way humans could possibly foresee. How ironic.

Like I said before, the people that give us something to lose are also the ones that give us everything to live for. The same goes for all the other connections we make with the world around us, from physical locations that hold nostalgic memories to worn out clothes that managed to see the next decade somehow. That's part of the reason I'm not turned off at the idea of being healthy past 100...those connections that are built over a lifetime transcend even death. They serve as motivation to find peace in what I'll eventually have to let go of, and nurture whatever I live to see born in its place. Being able to bear witness to how it all plays out, both the good and bad, is something I want to take solace in for as long as I can.

At some point, whether we verbalize it or not, we all feel how death influences our interactions with this plane of existence. In many different ways, we contend with the finality of everything on a daily basis. What's interesting is when you think about it, such finality is just as fragile as life in a universe of things looming to bring us closer to it. When we accept it for everything it is in all its filth is when it holds little weight over us. Life on earth has only really existed for a moment, but it's only taken a moment for us to see how precious all life is both leading to its end and thereafter. That which transcends death and rebirth, those moments of peace and clarity among a chaotic world, the ones we make a point to always remember, I think those moments are kind of like what you look for in the eye of a perfect storm. To make it there at all is a sight few experience in a lifetime, yet one every breed of human strives for nonetheless.

The One True Multiverse

You know, there are plenty of lengthy, profound ways to describe the nature of reality, and the universe we live in, most of which you'll find are fairly thought provoking both philosophically and scientifically. Yet, at its core it's probably not surprising I think reality is multifaceted far beyond human comprehension. Funnily enough that's not necessarily a flaw with humanity so much as it is a gift for us. If you understood every layer to every secret there is to know, life would get quite boring after a while now wouldn't it? Where's the fun in exploration, or in learning and growing if you already know what to expect at every turn?

It's really no secret though that the modern idea for *alternate* realities has become more and more popular for explaining certain phenomena over the past 20 years or so. Everything from black hole theories, to superhero conflicts, to the normalization of quantum physics have introduced the average Joe to the concept of a multiverse. The general idea being that the universe as we know it is only one of many, with parallel ones existing almost identically, but with minute differences compared to our universe, through space and time. Traditionally the idea speculates on alternate versions of earth and all of us on it. Imagine two universes where your life played out exactly the same, but in one you walk into a store to buy a winning lotto ticket, and in the other you decide to skip it and just go home for the night. Of course there are the big questions like, "what does a world where the Nazis won look like?" (Which is literally a TV show by the way), or "What if JFK was never killed?" As you can probably guess, much of our digital/technological breakthroughs have helped give way to this, yet another reason why this era in history is so important. In some aspects, it's easy to view such a concept as fanciful thinking, both on the entertainment *and* scientific level. Yet I actually think regardless of either thought arena, the developing models for a multiverse are pretty astounding given their implications in modern day.

As humankind reinvents itself, I think people are becoming more enamored with the possibilities for alternate simulations, both in the way of growth and adventure in life. If that's the case, I can't help but be fascinated at what a true multiverse looks like if we're thinking about it rationally. For one thing, If I'm to grossly generalize known physics, then it'd be somewhat accurate to say most multiverse theories revolve around the superposition of particles comprising the universe, which basically refers to them existing in multiple states simultaneously until they're observed or measured in nature. That principle is then applied to possibilities in reality as a whole, resulting in the idea that those multiple states, and thereby outcomes, all exist in their own planes of existence respectively, parallel to one another.

That being said, I'm *definitely* not a scientist or someone with credentials to assert such theories, but I believe a useful postulation to perceive the presence of a multiverse is best viewed as a thought experiment of sorts. To start off with, it helps to imagine the whole system as a cycle. When considering the natural progression of this universe's timeline—everything from the exact moment of its birth to the exact moment your eyes are following this text—exists as *one* singular passage of events. Everything from stars forming to planetary orbits being established, along with all their consequences, took place along one timeline. The idea that time moves in one direction like an arrow is nothing new, and its popular thinking to believe any changes to the past influences the present, but when you consider the connective nature of time and space itself, I dont think it's a stretch to argue that *any* deviation from what's already happened in this universe would result in its own, *distinct*, timeline, and thus its own, *distinct* universe.

Think about it. An effect can't be influenced by a change to its cause once said effect has come to pass. So no, stopping your parents from meeting wouldn't wipe you out of existence at all, considering, well, you already exist. You being born is already a completed event the universe has moved on from. It's not a static event that can be manipulated temporally. I'm pointing this out because any possible deviation that *could* exist in the progression of our known universe not only *would* exist in its *own* universe, but actually does exist simultaneously through spacetime. Now, as weird and out there as that hot take sounds, I think it's the kind of thought experiment that's worth playing with. Understand when I say this, I'm talking about literally every possible moment in time. Take a recognizable moment from the present day. A choice between wearing a red shirt and a green shirt for example. Regardless of which you choose, that means there exists a parallel reality *exactly* like ours, except the *only* difference up until the present moment in time is that you decided to wear the opposite color shirt. Through this thinking, it's easy to see how relevant probability is in all of this. But it's not just recognizable outcomes that matter here. Even the slightest of potential deviance amongst any given variable, down to the very nanosecond, results in a distinct and unique universe. That means which way you may shift your foot, tilt your head, or even just breath funny, literally is its own reality. *Every* possible outcome for *every possible* moment in time and space exists simultaneously.

I think the easiest way of picturing this is by imagining you have an infinity mirror. When there are two mirror images facing each other, the infinite reflections are always off by just a slight degree, so the line of images you see are all the same, but the farther back you look, the images become more distorted and foreign. Obviously there's a scientific explanation as to how this happens based on light, but it makes for a good analogy. Now imagine that every image represents a possible outcome down to the very instant it happens. As you go down the line, the realities you'd see would gradually start to differ, as the minute differences in each would become more drastic the further away you move from your *known* reality, so that's what I mean when I say they all exist simultaneously.

Under that thinking, one could conclude that if this applies to every moment in time, then a true multiverse would need to exist in an infinite cycle. Why a cycle? Well if all possible outcomes exist, then the order of events from creation to expansion to decay, would also have to exist simultaneously through every moment in time as well. In the same way an alternate universe exists right now where you choose a green shirt instead of a red shirt because it's a potential reality, one also exists where a version of the universe has already reached its end, and likewise one that's experiencing its creation at this very moment. Every other possible reality, like ones comparable to mirror images, fill in the rest of that circle. Another way of looking at it is if you had a cluster of bubbles where the big ones pop out of existence while smaller ones form and expand at the same time.

So! Obviously I'm not a scientist and obviously none of this is to be taken as scientific consensus. Although, like I said, there are plenty of *real* theories similar to this. Regardless, it's still worth putting out here because of the philosophical implications tied to it. Believing that the multiverse functions in such a way is easy when you assume everything I laid out is all wrong to begin with, mainly because I have no concern with being right. My concern is looking at how we rationally conceptualize possibility and analyze probability. I think when you really ponder it, there's little denying the endless links between the natural, human condition, and the countless possibilities we envision for ourselves as it develops. Suppose for a moment there actually is no such thing as a multiverse, and it's all just hearsay. Even if every conceivable theory is completely false, earth is inherently a blank canvas for life, and our imaginations are projections of who and what we could be in it. The fact of the matter is, our minds innately create simulations for both how we *want* reality to play out, and how we *expect* it to. We do this every second of every day, about as consciously as breathing at that. In our everyday actions, we allow certain visions to come to fruition, while rejecting others. Everything from deciding you'll stay in this weekend, eat comfort food and watch reruns of The Office, to deciding that in ten years' time you'll be self-employed with a happy family by your side. Those ideas in our minds are pictures that, while animated in some retrospect, remain as frozen images of reality for us to aspire for. They're visions that manifest digitally in our virtual worlds like video game genres, aesthetically in the different tones and voices of our art and music, and linguistically through literature and the infinite stories we pass on and refine through generations. Even the most fictional, whimsical tales of other worlds teach us something about the *real* world if you pay enough attention.

In other words, our essence of foresight helps us conceptualize alternate realities *all the time*, and often deliberate on whether to empower them or not. Quite the hidden ability of being human if you ask me. Or perhaps *underrated* is a better word.

Now then, let's assume that I'm right for a second. In a multiverse where every outcome persists, where's the meaning in anything if it already exists elsewhere? It's something I asked myself in thinking about this and, honestly, it's pretty simple. In the same way an infinity mirror displays small nuance in its images, so does the reality we consider meaningful. It may seem like individual choice and free will serve no purpose in a system where *every* choice comes to fruition, but the circumstances surrounding said choices are far more complicated than we could ever imagine. Sure, knowing that a given outcome already persisted in another universe may seem like the one you're experiencing is pointless, but it's actually the opposite. Even as a species aware of so many possibilities in the universe, we only get a chance at truly *experiencing* a *fraction* of it firsthand. That's because even if you knew that every reality happens somewhere, humans are inherently unequipped to comprehend *all* of them. That level of knowledge just isn't possible. As a result, there's only so much of existence we can truly perceive that has meaning to us at all. Your experiences, and your stream of consciousness, as similar as it would be to another version of yourself making all the opposite choices in your life, or even a version of you living the life you've always dreamt of, is, well, still distinct. It's still uniquely yours, and still has value as a life connected to everything. In an infinite system like this one, nothing truly repeats. Everything matters, it's just hard to wrap our heads around sometimes.

Objectively speaking, the laws of physics limit us, and given the nature of humanity, I'd say rightfully so. Regardless, there's no denying that the fabric of reality, *any* reality, is inherently fragile. Fragile and yet, still one of the most beautiful essences that can be shaped by humans. It's like glass, or water in a way. Both can have their images distorted easily, as it's easy to pollute water, and easy to break glass to the point where everything shatters apart beyond repair. In our physical universe there are so many *insanely* specific scientific conditions required for life on earth to exist, period, and so many insanely *catastrophic* consequences for if any of those conditions are even slightly skewed or altered. I think people are starting to understand this more clearly as time goes on, even if we don't always verbalize it. We realize, not just as humans, but as *people*, that even our smallest actions, especially in such technologically charged times, have far greater influence on the immediate world and the many systems in it than we initially realized. It's true in a social sense, political sense, psychological sense, economic sense, environmental sense. You name it.

Honestly, I'd personally like to imagine if a true multiverse exists, it works in the way I've described here, but I'd be lying if I said it's not because of my own nerdiness and how the thought of such a system makes sense to me. If it does become testable someday and I'm off though, admittedly I'd like to hope at least *part* of my hypothetical scenario was right. Regardless, for now the multiverse is an illusion we interact with on a daily basis, and through that, it becomes reality. In that way, it's simultaneously fact and fiction. Both the most rational human thought and baseless human intuition. The one *true* multiverse however is the one we create and enable as humans. In many ways we have the choice to embrace or reject infinite versions of what to be in our world and universe. Through everything we've already managed to build in this life, we get to look at what we could *truly do* with all the untapped potential of humankind. Whether there's a multiverse or not, an innate network of possibility, changing form across eons is what drives us in many ways.

In the end, as structured as science may be, even the greatest minds need some imagination to think outside the box toward something new. It's finding a balance in the relationship between our reality and these abstract concepts that make life worthwhile. Like I said, we've been doing it since the beginning, so why stop now?

Don't miss out!

Visit the website below and you can sign up to receive emails whenever Justin Reynolds publishes a new book. There's no charge and no obligation.

https://books2read.com/r/B-A-BGUM-QDKKB

BOOKS2READ

Connecting independent readers to independent writers.

About the Author

Justin Reynolds is a certified observer of humanity who often participates, which means you've probably never heard of him considering that's not a real credential! He has traveled extensively across the world garnering experience and insight on things most people think about at 2 am when they can't sleep, so he decided to write a book about it, hoping someone may find his opinion useful. He enjoys cooking, running, martial arts, and obviously writing.

www.ingramcontent.com/pod-product-compliance
Lightning Source LLC
Chambersburg PA
CBHW031355040426
42444CB00005B/306